The Duchess of Malfi

THE NEW MERMAIDS

General Editor

BRIAN GIBBONS

Professor of English Literature, University of Münster

The Duchess of Malfi

JOHN WEBSTER

Edited by

ELIZABETH M. BRENNAN

Emeritus Reader in English
University of London

LONDON/A & C BLACK

NEW YORK/W W NORTON

Third edition 1993
A & C Black (Publishers) Limited
35 Bedford Row, London WC1R 4JH

ISBN 0–7136-3754-4

© 1993 A & C Black (Publishers) Limited

First published in this form 1964
Second edition 1983
Ernest Benn Limited

© 1983 Ernest Benn Limited

Published in the United States of America
by W. W. Norton & Company Inc.
500 Fifth Avenue, New York, NY 10110
ISBN 0–393-90066-5 (USA)

A CIP catalogue record for this book
is available from the British Library.

Filmset in Plantin by
Selwood Systems, Midsomer Norton
Printed and bound in Great Britain by
Biddles Limited, Guildford and King's Lynn

TO
ERIC

CONTENTS

ACKNOWLEDGEMENTS

IN. THE PREPARATION of this edition I am indebted to those previous editors whose names are listed in the Abbreviations. In particular I should like to acknowledge the debts that I owe to F. L. Lucas's edition of Webster; to Dr J. R. Brown's bibliographical studies of the play, and to the critical work of Dr Gunnar Boklund and Professor Clifford Leech. I am also grateful to the General Editor of the Series, Professor Philip Brockbank, for his sympathetic criticism and guidance.

ELIZABETH M. BRENNAN

First edition

In 1963, when I undertook to edit *The Duchess of Malfi* for the New Mermaids, I had had only one opportunity to see the play, in the Stratford-on-Avon Company's 1960 production at the Aldwych Theatre, with Peggy Ashcroft as the Duchess. Though some have irritated me, none of the major productions or distinguished actors whose work in them I have seen in the last thirty years has failed to provide the impetus to reread Webster's drama in the light of its impact in the theatre.

For most of this period I taught in the University of London, and it is a pleasure to be able to thank colleagues for pertinent comments and former students for the occasionally impertinent remarks which have made me reconsider my views of John Webster's Duchess. Among critics, M.C. Bradbrook has been a perennial source of wisdom; to Lee Bliss, John Russell Brown, Charles Forker and Lisa Jardine I am indebted for fresh insights. John Chalker, Peter Dixon, Inga-Stina Ewbank, David Gunby, Harold Jenkins, Laurie Maguire and Richard Proudfoot have provided the stimuli of encouragement, example and help.

Lastly (without wrong last to be named) my husband, Eric Lowden, has supplied the constant and practical support without which this revision would not have been completed. In gratitude I dedicate the work to him.

ELIZABETH M. BRENNAN

Third edition

ABBREVIATIONS

Apart from the works in the following list, full titles and publication details of works referred to in the Introduction and notes are given when they are first cited.

Shakespearean quotations and references are taken from *William Shakespeare: The Complete Works*, edited by Peter Alexander (1951; reprinted 1973). Quotations from *The White Devil* and *The Devil's Law-Case* are taken from the New Mermaids texts, edited by Elizabeth M. Brennan (1966; 1975).

The following are used in addition to the abbreviations listed in *The Concise Oxford Dictionary*:

Anderson	Marcia Lee Anderson, as cited by R.W. Dent
BL	The British Library
Bowers II	*The Dramatic Works of Thomas Dekker*, edited by Fredson Bowers, volume II (Cambridge, 1955)
Brereton	J. Le Gay Brereton, 'Webster's Twin Masterpieces', *Elizabethan Drama: Notes and Studies* (Sydney, 1909)
Brown	*The Duchess of Malfi*, edited by John Russell Brown, The Revels Plays (London, 1964)
conj.	conjecture
Dent	R. W. Dent, *John Webster's Borrowing* (Berkeley and Los Angeles: University of California Press, 1960)
Dyce	*The Works of John Webster*, edited by Alexander Dyce (revised edition, London, 1857)
ed.	editorial
ed. cit.	in the edition cited
edn	edition
Forker	Charles R. Forker, *Skull Beneath the Skin: The Achievement of John Webster* (Carbondale and Edwardsville: Southern Illinois University Press, 1986)
Gunby	*John Webster: Three Plays*, edited by D. C. Gunby, The Penguin English Library (Harmondsworth, 1972)
Hazlitt	*The Dramatic Works of John Webster*, edited by W. C. Hazlitt (London, 1857)
H&S	*Ben Jonson* edited by C. H. Herford and Percy and Evelyn Simpson, 11 vols (Oxford, 1925–52)
Lucas	*The Complete Works of John Webster*, edited by F. L. Lucas, 4 vols (London, 1927; reprinted 1966)
Lucas II	'The Duchess of Malfi', *The Complete Works of John Webster*, volume II

McIlwraith	'The Duchess of Malfi', *Five Stuart Tragedies*, edited by A. K. McIlwraith, The World's Classics (London, 1953)
McLuskie and Uglow	*John Webster, The Duchess of Malfi*, edited by Kathleen McLuskie and Jennifer Uglow, Plays in Performance (Bristol, 1989)
MRE	Manchester Royal Exchange Theatre
n.	note
n.s.	new series
NT	National Theatre
OED	*The Oxford English Dictionary*
Q1	the quarto of 1623 (BL copies: 644.f.72; Ashley 2207)
Q1a	uncorrected state of Q1
Q1b	corrected state of Q1
Q1c	second corrected state of Q1, found only in sheet G outer forme: in this edition III.ii. 110–40, 201–73; III. iii. 2–31. See J. R. Brown's list in 'The Printing of John Webster's Plays (II)', *SB* 8 (1956), 117–20.
Q2	the quarto of 1640 (BL copies: 82.c.26 (3); 642.k.42)
Q3	the quarto of 1678 (BL copy 163.k.65)
Q4	the quarto of 1708, entitled *The Unfortunate Dutchess of Malfy or the Unnatural Brothers* (BL copy 644.i.71)
Qq	quartos
RSC	Royal Shakespeare Company
Sampson	*The White Devil* and *The Duchess of Malfi*, edited by Martin W. Sampson, The Belles Lettres Series (London, 1904)
s.d.	stage direction
s.p.	speech prefix
Vaughan	*The Duchess of Malfi*, edited by C. Vaughan, The Temple Dramatists (London, 1896)

Periodicals and serial publications

CahE	*Cahiers Élisabéthains*
CompD	*Comparative Drama*
DramaS	*Drama Survey*
EIC	*Essays in Criticism*
ElizT	*Elizabethan Theatre*
ELH	*English Literary History*
ELN	*English Language Notes*
ELR	*English Language Review*
ES	*English Studies*
ESA	*English Studies in Africa*
G	*Genre*
JEGP	*Journal of English and Germanic Philology*
L&Psy	*Literature and Psychology*
MLR	*Modern Language Review*
MLS	*Modern Language Studies*

MRev	*Malahat Review*
N&Q	*Notes & Queries*
PMLA	*Publications of the Modern Language Association of America*
PQ	*Philological Quarterly*
RenD	*Renaissance Drama*
RES	*Review of English Studies*
RORD	*Research Opportunities in Renaissance Drama*
SB	*Studies in Bibliography*
SEL	*Studies in English Literature*
ShS	*Shakespeare Survey*
SUAS	*Stratford-upon-Avon Studies*
TD	*Themes in Drama*
TLS	*Times Literary Supplement*
TRI	*Theatre Research International*
TSLL	*Texas Studies in Literature and Language*
YES	*Yearbook of English Studies*

INTRODUCTION

THE AUTHOR

JOHN WEBSTER was born *c.* 1578–79, the eldest son of the owner of a business engaged in the making, hiring and selling of coaches, wagons and carts in Cow Lane.[1] Living in the Smithfield area of London, the family belonged to St Sepulcre's parish. As no Coachmakers' Company was incorporated till 1677, John Webster senior and, later, his son Edward became freemen of the Merchant Taylors' Company, whose school John Webster almost certainly attended before passing to the New Inn and being admitted to the Middle Temple on 1 August 1598. The width of his reading in classical and modern authors and his method of dramatic composition reveal a studious mind; his plays contain trial scenes and many legal allusions. His family's concern in practical aspects of mounting entertainments – his father is known to have supplied transport both to players and for shows or pageants between 1591 and 1613 – no doubt combined with Webster's own experience of Inns of Court Revels to produce an active interest in the theatre. He had a share in *Arches of Triumph*, a Coronation entertainment of 1604, and in 1624 composed a Lord Mayor's Pageant, *Monuments of Honour*, describing himself on the title-page as 'Iohn Webster, Merchant-Taylor'. Though 'born free' of the Merchant Taylors' Company – that is, he had an inherited right to become a freeman, upon reaching his majority and paying a fee (as distinct from serving as an apprentice) – he did not exercise this right until 1615. Two years later Henry Fitzgeffrey, in *Notes from Blackfriars, Satyres and Satyricall Epigrams*, expressed some doubt about the dramatist's true profession:

> ... Crabbed (*Websterio*)
> The *Play-wright, Cart-wright*: whether? either!

The satirist had no doubt, however, about including Webster among typical frequenters of the Blackfriars theatre. The family business was also mentioned by William Heminges in a mock elegy for the loss of Thomas Randolph's little finger in an affray of 1632:

> ... websters brother would nott lend a Coach:
> He swore that all weare hired to Conuey
> The Malfy dutches sadly on her way.

---

[1] The fullest modern account of Webster's life will be found in Forker, pp. 3–61.

The earliest records of John Webster's employment as a dramatist are found in the diary – more properly an account book – of the theatre manager and financier Philip Henslowe who, in 1602, paid Webster, together with Anthony Munday, Thomas Middleton, Thomas Dekker, Henry Chettle, Thomas Heywood, Michael Drayton and Wentworth Smith, for work on *Caesar's Fall* and *Christmas Comes but Once a Year* – both now lost – and *Lady Jane*, a two-part play which probably survives, reconstructed and shortened, in *The Famous History of Sir Thomas Wyatt* (1607).[2]

In 1604 Webster wrote the Induction and, probably, the part of Passarello for *The Malcontent*, a tragicomedy by John Marston who, though the same age as Webster, had entered the Middle Temple *c.* 1595. Two city comedies, *Westward Ho!* and *Northward Ho!*, written by Webster and Dekker for Paul's Boys, were performed in 1604 and 1605. His address to the reader of his first tragedy, *The White Devil*, performed and published in 1612, expresses admiration for Heywood, to whose *Apology for Actors* he contributed a commendatory poem in the same year, as well as for Dekker, Shakespeare, Beaumont, Fletcher and the scholarly dramatists George Chapman and Ben Jonson.[3] Webster also refers to the play's unsympathetic reception, despite which his second tragedy, *The Duchess of Malfi*, seems to have followed it quickly since some of its material was derived from sources published in 1612. Though the play cannot have been completed before late 1612, it must have been performed before December 1614, the date of the death of William Ostler, the actor who first played Antonio Bologna.

A Monumental Column, Webster's elegy on the death of Prince Henry, the heir to the throne, appeared in 1613. The sixth edition of Sir Thomas Overbury's *Characters* (1615) contained thirty-two new 'characters' including those of 'An Excellent Actor', 'A Reverent Judge' and 'An Ordinarie Widdow' which are attributed to Webster.[4] In the epistle dedicatory of his tragicomedy *The Devil's Law-Case*, dated *c.* 1617,[5] Webster mentions a play called *Guise* of whose date and genre nothing certain is known.[6] In September 1624 Webster, Dekker, William Rowley and John Ford quickly wrote *The Late Murder of the Son upon the Mother, or Keep the Widow Waking*, a play we only know about through the

---

[2] For this information I am indebted to Laurie Maguire and *The Dramatic Works of Thomas Dekker*, edited by Fredson Bowers, volume I (Cambridge, 1953), pp. 399–400n.

[3] See Elizabeth M. Brennan, ' "An Understanding Auditory": An Audience for John Webster', in *John Webster*, edited by Brian Morris, Mermaid Critical Commentaries (London, 1970), pp. 3–19.

[4] See Dent, p. 59.

[5] Ibid.

[6] See R. G. Howarth, 'Webster's "Guise" ', *N&Q* n.s. 13 (1966), 294–95; Forker, pp. 134–35.

Proceedings of the Court of Star Chamber,[7] for no text survives, though it was acted often. On 29 October 1624, the Guild of Merchant Taylors celebrated the inauguration of one of their members, Sir John Gore, as Lord Mayor of London with a pageant prepared by John Webster, the pageant wagons for which were probably supplied by his brother Edward. It cost them over £1,000: 'a greater sum than they had ever spent for such a purpose in three centuries.'[8]

Webster may have had a collaborating hand in Middleton's comedy *Anything for a Quiet Life*,[9] *c.* 1620–21, and *The Fair Maid of the Inn*, which was licensed for production in 1626 and printed in the Beaumont and Fletcher first folio in 1647.[10] The dates of his other extant plays are uncertain.[11] Probably between 1624 and 1625 he collaborated with Rowley and perhaps Heywood on the comedy *A Cure for a Cuckold*, and wrote some part of the minor tragedy *Appius and Virginia*. Though he was the author of some occasional verses, Webster seems to have written no other plays, and it is presumed that he died in the 1630s.

THE SOURCES OF THE PLAY

Like Vittoria Corombona, the heroine of *The White Devil*, the Duchess of Malfi was an historical figure. Born Giovanna d'Aragona, she was married in 1490, at about twelve years of age, to Alfonso Piccolomini, son and heir of the first Duke of Amalfi. He succeeded to the dukedom in 1493, but died of gout in 1498. The Duchess, aged about nineteen, already had a daughter, Caterina. Her son was born posthumously in 1499 and succeeded to the dukedom, which she ruled for him, as regent. Despite French and Spanish invasions the state flourished. The Duchess was able to pay off debts incurred by her husband and live prosperously.

Antonio Bologna, who came of a reputable family, was brought up at the court of Naples. He became major-domo to Federico, the state's last Aragonian King, and followed his master into exile in France. Upon Federico's death in 1504 Antonio returned to Naples, where he was offered the post of major-domo in the household of the Duchess of Malfi, who was herself a member of the house of Aragon. The young widow fell quickly and passionately in love with Antonio. Fearing the wrath of her brothers – Lodovico, who had resigned his title of Marquis of Gerace to become a Cardinal, and Carlo (Webster's Ferdinand), who

---

[7] See C. J. Sisson, *Lost Plays of Shakespeare's Age* (Cambridge, 1936), pp. 80–124.

[8] Forker, pp. 164–65

[9] Ibid., pp. 145–59

[10] Ibid., pp. 189–200

[11] Ibid., pp. 171–224

had succeeded to it – she married Antonio in secret, with her waiting-woman as sole witness to the ceremony.

In real life, as in Webster's play, their marriage was successfully concealed for some years. The birth of their first child was undetected, but the birth of a second caused rumours which, reaching the ears of the Aragonian brothers, led them to set spies to watch their sister. Antonio took his two children to Ancona, leaving the Duchess, who was again pregnant, in her palace. Unbearably lonely, she found an excuse to set out with a great retinue on pilgrimage to Loretto, from whence she proceeded to join Antonio. Upon her arrival in Ancona, she revealed her marriage to her household, and declared that she would renounce her rank and title to live privately with Antonio and their children. One of her astonished servants set out to inform the Cardinal what had happened; the rest deserted her and returned to Amalfi.

At Ancona, where their third child was born, the Duchess and her husband were allowed only a few months' peace before the Cardinal of Aragon put pressure on Cardinal Gonzaga, Legate of Ancona, to banish Antonio. Having foreseen this, Antonio had made preparations to take refuge with a friend in Siena. As soon as the decree of his banishment was issued – in the summer of 1511 – he set out with the Duchess and their children, thus evading any attempt that might have been made to capture or murder them. The Cardinal continuing to exert his influence against them, the head of the Signiory of Siena was persuaded by his brother, Cardinal Petrucci, to expel them. This time Antonio and his family did not depart so quickly. On their way to Venice they were overtaken by armed horsemen. By asserting that her brothers would not harm her in person, the Duchess was able to persuade Antonio to escape with their eldest child, a boy of six or seven years of age. They arrived safely in Milan, probably in the late summer of 1512. There is no evidence to connect the Aragonian brothers with the death of the Duchess, but after being taken back to her palace in Amalfi, neither she, her two youngest children nor her waiting-woman were ever seen again.

Not knowing what had happened to them, Antonio lived in Milan: first under the protection of Silvio Savelli; later in the households of the Marchese di Bitonto and Alfonso Visconti. Though his wife's brothers had confiscated his property in Naples, Antonio still hoped to appease them. Perhaps they held out promises of restoring the Duchess to him. He was frequently warned that his life was in danger, one warning coming from a man called Delio, who had heard Antonio's story from a Neapolitan friend. On an October day in 1513, Delio and a companion passed Antonio, who looked dismayed, with two servants on their way to mass at the church of S. Francesco. A few minutes later an uproar was heard. Looking back, Delio and his friend saw that Antonio had been stabbed to death by a Lombard captain called Daniele de Bozolo and three accomplices. All four escaped.

The diary of Giacomo the Notary, of Naples, records the stir caused by the Duchess's leaving Amalfi to go on pilgrimage to Loretto and by her subsequent revelation of her marriage to her major-domo. The Corona group of manuscripts in the Biblioteca Nazionale in Naples contains accounts of her life, originally collected in the sixteenth century and copied out and augmented by later writers up to the eighteenth century. Behind these manuscripts lies the twenty-sixth of the first part of Matteo Bandello's *Novelle* (1554). The manuscript accounts contain more details of Neapolitan interest than Bandello's narrative, but only one version is obviously independent of his.[12]

The novella includes both imagined dialogue and material based on hearsay. Yet it is sufficiently accurate in outline to warrant the assumption that Bandello, who wrote sonnets under the name of Delio, was the same Delio who had known Antonio Bologna, having heard his story in Milan, and who had witnessed his death.

Bandello relates the tragic story without moral comment but, since his introduction decries murders which are motivated by a desire to avenge wounded honour, condemnation of the Aragonian brothers is implicit. The French writer François de Belleforest is more outspoken. At the end of his account, the first in his second tome of *Histoires Tragiques*, the reader's sympathy may be with the murdered Duchess, the victim of her brothers' cruelty, but in the course of his narration Belleforest frequently exclaims against her, presenting her as a lascivious widow who is unable to live without a man; who forgets her noble blood to run after one beneath her station and commits an execrable impiety in feigning a pilgrimage to Loretto. This version, with its moral comment, was printed in English by William Painter in his *Second Tome of the Palace of Pleasure* (1567). Thomas Beard, in *The Theatre of God's Judgments* (1597), treated the Duchess's history under the heading 'Of whoredomes committed vnder Colour of Marriage'. The tone of accounts of the marriage given by George Whetstone in *An Heptameron of Civil Discourses* (1582) and Simon Goulart, whose version was translated in Edward Grimeston's *Admirable and Memorable Histories* (1607), is also condemnatory. Only in brief references in H.C.'s *The Forest of Fancy* (1579) and Robert Greene's *Gwydonius, the Card of Fancy* (1584) is the Duchess's choice of husband commended.

Painter's version of Bandello was probably Webster's main source. Some details of action, such as the mental torture of the Duchess and the echo scene, and some parts of the dialogue are derived from the story of Musidorus and Pamela in Sir Philip Sidney's *Arcadia*. There are slight indications that Webster knew Bandello's novella in the original

---

[12] See Gunnar Boklund, *'The Duchess of Malfi': Sources, Themes, Characters* (Cambridge, MA: Harvard University Press 1962), pp. 9–11.

Italian, and he may have read – or seen – Lope de Vega's tragedy *El Mayordomo de la Duquesa de Amalfi*, which was not published till 1618.[13]

STRUCTURE, THEMES AND IMAGERY

The Duchess of Malfi, like *The White Devil*, has the dramatic framework of the revenge play – popular on the English stage from 1588 to 1642 – though it contains fewer of the trappings of this genre. The echo from the Duchess's tomb fulfils one of the functions of the ghost of revenge tragedy by warning a doomed man of his danger, while at the same time revealing the unknown fact of its own death. Dumb show is used for both the Cardinal's investiture as a soldier and the Duchess's banishment. The play's climax, comprehending the poisoning of Julia, accidental or mistaken murders, and the repeated stabbings of the last scene, produces enough corpses to make it comparable with the gory dramas of the 1590s. The conventions of madness and the masque are combined in the dance of madmen which forms part of the complicated mental torture to which the Duchess is subjected by Ferdinand.

Ferdinand's own madness takes the form of lycanthropy. Grounded in the animality of Ferdinand's nature, it becomes part of Webster's characterization of him. As a recognized symptom of love-melancholy, lycanthropy confirms the dramatist's presentation of Ferdinand as a jealous lover.[14] Within the plot, it enables Webster to incorporate an element of unpredictability in the final conflict.

Madness is also subtly treated in the characterization of the Duchess. Early in the play it is anticipated in some of Antonio's words (I.ii.337–41), which also adumbrate the later presentation of Ferdinand, and in the striking lines which Cariola speaks at the end of Act I:

> Whether the spirit of greatness, or of woman
> Reign most in her, I know not, but it shows
> A fearful madness: I owe her much of pity.   (I.ii.417–19)

In the fourth act the Duchess's madness is more powerful as a threat than in its brief and intermittent reality; there is no doubt of her sanity when the moment of death approaches.

Courtly Reward and Desert

One of the themes of *The Duchess of Malfi* is courtly reward, previously

---

[13] Ibid., pp. 1–74; see also John Loftis, 'Lope de Vega and Webster's Amalfi Plays', *CompD* 16 (1982), 64–78; Forker, p. 546, n. 27.

[14] See Elizabeth M. Brennan, 'The Relationship between Brother and Sister in the Plays of John Webster', *MLR* 58 (1963), 488–94; Forker, pp. 306–11 (especially his analysis of Ferdinand as a schizophrenic).

explored by Webster in *The White Devil*. Here, courtly reward is con-
trasted with courtly desert. As in *The White Devil*, the theme is introduced in the play's opening scene in the words of a man who has
received what he considers unjust treatment – a man who is destined to
be the villain hired to murder the heroine.

The opposition of courtly reward and courtly desert enforces the
ironies of the final action. The Cardinal who had indirectly bought
Bosola's life – in the sense of his life-work – tries vainly to buy his own
life at Bosola's hands. Bosola comments on this reversal by referring in
the same breath to the Cardinal's presumed profession of Christianity
and his real manifestation of corruption:

> Thy prayers and proffers
> Are both unseasonable.   (V.v.15–16)

The Cardinal cries for mercy; but Bosola reminds him:

> Pray, and be sudden: when thou kill'd'st thy sister,
> Thou took'st from Justice her most equal balance,
> And left her naught but her sword.   (V.v.38–40)

Though Bosola stabs him twice, it is Ferdinand who, in his madness,
kills his brother and gives Bosola his own death-wound. The Cardinal
acknowledges the justice of his own doom, while Bosola reaches the
climax of his courtly service in rewarding Ferdinand for his iniquity. As
he kills him, he rejoices:

> ... the last part of my life
> Hath done me best service.   (V.v.63–64)

Probably for the first time in his career, Bosola has stabbed a villain
instead of an innocent. The dying Cardinal has strength left to speak of
Bosola's death in terms which relate it to the reward that Bosola has so
long sought:

> Thou hast thy payment too.   (V.v.73)

Bosola, in turn, lives long enough to explain to Roderigo the reason for
the deaths that have occurred with such swift violence. Significantly, he
speaks not of reward, but of revenge: that revenge which is both a
human reward for injury and an instrument of divine vengeance for sin.
Revenge is Bosola's reward to Ferdinand for the neglect of his service
and distortion of his potential for good.

Ideas about courtly reward and desert are found in other passages of
the play, and constitute an important theme: one of the many which
Webster examines. Some, suggested by the action, are explicitly enun-
ciated in sententiae and philosophic utterances.[15]

---

[15] Discussions of Webster's philosophy, particularly as it is expressed in the
play's closing speeches, are listed below, pp. 136–37.

Confinement

A notable group of images is concerned with confinement, represented as a prison or a trap. The soul is seen as a prisoner of the body which will only be liberated in death. It is also like a caged bird, and the Duchess of Malfi is entrapped as men catch birds, with nets and cunning practices.

Webster approaches this concept indirectly and subtly. In hiring Bosola to spy on their sister, the Cardinal and Ferdinand are setting a trap; and as men trap wild creatures in order to kill them, so the Duchess, if caught, will be killed. Ferdinand's apparent warning –

> ... believe't,
> Your darkest actions: nay, your privat'st thoughts,
> Will come to light   (I.ii.234–36)

– and the Cardinal's comment on secret marriage –

> The marriage night
> Is the entrance into some prison   (I.ii.243–44)

– are not prophecies, but threats. Bosola's first task is to discover her secrets; his second is to secure her imprisonment.

Bosola's intelligencing takes years to produce the results required by her brothers, but their threats have an immediate fulfilment in the life of the Duchess: their determined wills and the atmosphere of her own poisoned court limit her activities. Her marriage ceremony is literally confined within the walls of her chamber. In this sense her marriage night *is* the entrance to a prison. Like a prisoner's, her movements and emotions are restricted.

The imagery of the wooing scene suggests, prophetically, not only restraint, but madness and violent death. Nevertheless, a happier instance of the image of confinement occurs in the Duchess's reply to Antonio's question about her brothers:

> Do not think of them:
> All discord, without this circumference,
> Is only to be pitied, and not fear'd.   (I.ii.383–85)

This may be interpreted as a reference to the wedding ring that she has given Antonio, or to the confinement of the wife's arms as she embraces her husband.[16]

---

[16] Commenting on this statement in 'The Ring and the Jewel in Webster's Tragedies', *TSLL* 14 (1972), 253–68, Samuel Schuman says that the Duchess's 'circumference' is 'surely *both* the wedding ring and the embrace' and Wayne A. Rebhorn, in 'Circle, Sword and the Futile Quest: The Nightmare World of Webster's *Duchess of Malfi*', *CahE* 27 (1985), 53–66, says that there is no reason why 'the word could not be taken as a more general reference, accompanied by a sweeping gesture, to the room and hence to the palace ...'

The idea of betrayal through violent entrapment is present in Antonio's recognition, after the birth of his first child, that Bosola is trying to undermine him. The concept of something precious being contained in something frail, parallel to that of the soul being imprisoned in the body, is reflected in Ferdinand's cry:

> Foolish men,
> That e'er will trust their honour in a bark,
> Made of so slight, weak bulrush, as is woman,
> Apt every minute to sink it!   (II.v.33–36)

When her brothers know that the Duchess and Antonio have fallen into the trap of a secret marriage Ferdinand goes to take them both in her lodgings.[17] Their married happiness is seen to include Antonio's teasing, which leads to his leaving his wife alone. So the poniard which might have killed Antonio is presented by Ferdinand as a warning – or as a hint to commit suicide – to Antonio's wife. Ignoring the hint, the Duchess plans to secure life and liberty, first for her husband, and then for herself and their children. In doing so she rashly accepts Bosola's advice, which is itself a snare. He suggests a feigned pilgrimage, but the Duchess and her family make a properly pious devotion at the shrine of Our Lady of Loretto; her brother the Cardinal, on the contrary, resigns his religious vestments to be accoutred as a soldier before banishing the Duchess and her family. Witnessed by pilgrims who comment on his cruel bearing, the Cardinal vents his rage upon his sister by tearing off her wedding ring.

Having taken the Duchess in her flight, Bosola taunts her with the question that reveals his own treachery:

> ⌈   ... I would have you tell me whether
> Is that note worse that frights the silly birds

(p. 54). Both rings may be visible in the mind of a scholar, in the study, but the actor portraying the Duchess can only indicate one on stage. Though some have illustrated the circumference by an indication of the ring, an embrace strengthens the parallel between the Duchess's wooing of Antonio and Julia's courtship of Bosola: see V.ii.161–62. McLuskie and Uglow indicate that this has been a stage interpretation since 1850 (p. 91), though, in the 1980 MRE production, 'Helen Mirren gave a different point to the geometric image by holding wide her arms to look like the Renaissance emblem of a man inside the circle of the world' (ibid., p. 93). See also Christina Luckyj, *A Winter's Snake: Dramatic Form in the Tragedies of John Webster* (Athens and London: University of Georgia Press, 1989), pp. 48–49.

[17] In fact, Ferdinand behaves as if he were a cuckold going to trap his wife and a lover: see Brennan, 'Relationship', p. 493.

Out of the corn; or that which doth allure them
To the nets? You have heark'ned to the last too much.

(III.v.98–101)

Bosola is vizarded when he says this, so that his boast loses its force and appears instead as a mysterious reflection on an otherwise unknown plan. The idea of the Duchess as a trapped bird is later underlined by the way Ferdinand toys with her before having her killed. Immediately after being captured she asks Bosola to what prison she must go, but he insists that her brothers mean her safety and pity. The Duchess knows better:

Pity!
With such a pity men preserve alive
Pheasants and quails, when they are not fat enough
To be eaten. (III.v.108–11)

Shortly afterwards the trapping net becomes a symbol of necessary evil which will reveal good: just as death is an evil which, at the Last Judgement, will reveal the good of the soul. This appears in the conclusion of the Duchess's fable of the Salmon and the Dogfish:

'O', quoth the Salmon, 'sister, be at peace:
Thank Jupiter, we have both pass'd the Net,
Our value never can be truly known,
Till in the Fisher's basket we be shown;
I'th' Market then my price may be the higher,
Even when I am nearest to the Cook, and fire.' (III.v.133–38)

Q1's capitalization suggests a parabolic interpretation: the Fisher is God; the gathering in of the fishes is a harvest at which not wheat and tares, but good and bad fish are to be judged; the Market is the Judgement; the Cook is another symbol for God; the fire represents hell fire: at the Judgement one is as close to hell as to the joys of heaven. The whole passage is a comment on the difference between divine and human estimation of worth. Thus it is related to the theme of reward and desert, while the attitude of the Dogfish to rank is one of the play's comments on princes and their courts.

Images of imprisonment occur most frequently in Act IV. The Duchess's treatment within her own palace suggests that she is confined as a punishment and restrained as if she were mad. Cariola assures her that she will live 'to shake this durance off', but the Duchess's mind turns again to contemplate the snared bird – which is how Bosola has taught her to think of herself.

The robin red-breast and the nightingale
Never live long in cages. (IV.ii.13–14)

Earlier, the Duchess had envied the birds' ability to

> ... choose their mates,
> And carol their sweet pleasures to the spring.   (III.v.19–20)

Later, Bosola's exhortation to her encapsulates the play's prison imagery:

> Thou art a box of worm seed, at best, but a salvatory of green mummy: what's this flesh? a little cruded milk, fantastical puff-paste: our bodies are weaker than those paper prisons boys use to keep flies in: more contemptible; since ours is to preserve earth-worms: didst thou ever see a lark in a cage? such is the soul in the body: this world is like her little turf of grass, and the heaven o'er our heads, like her looking-glass, only gives us a miserable knowledge of the small compass of our prison.   (IV.ii.123–31)

The final symbol of the Duchess of Malfi's confinement is the coffin itself: her 'last presence chamber'. Her final thought is of a confinement that leads immediately to liberty. So she halts her executioners for an instant:

> Yet stay, heaven gates are not so highly arch'd
> As princes' palaces: they that enter there
> Must go upon their knees.   (IV.ii.228–30)

'Strait is the gate and narrow is the way.' The implied contrast is with the space, the broad way, that leads to perdition.

Though the Duchess dies in Act IV, the image which has hitherto been so closely associated with her persists. Bosola, who had ensnared her for her brothers, is able to confine the Cardinal to the room in which the Duchess's death is to be avenged. So caught, the Cardinal cries,

> Shall I die like a leveret
> Without any resistance?   (V.v.44–45)

Webster's Theatre Language

Action, imagery and characterization in *The Duchess of Malfi* incorporate contrasts, parallels, paradoxes and inversions of the norm. The brothers who should love the Duchess are her most cruel enemies; the husband who should give her strength has to take courage from her example. The most complicated presentation of the conflict between appearance and reality is found in Bosola, in whom it is made visible through his use of disguise, though that is less important than the invisible disguising of his true nature at the beginning of the play, and his conversion, after the Duchess's murder, at the end.

The death of the Duchess suggests that the darkness of evil extinguishes the light of good, but thereby liberates the good, fair soul from its cage and paper prison into the light of eternity. It is Bosola who is left in 'this sensible hell' where, despite conversion, he is unable to prevent himself from killing the goodness which is represented by Antonio.

Themes of *The White Devil* are echoed in Webster's later tragedy, indicating his continuing concern with the corruption of princely courts and of great men. Both tragedies provide, through their action, an opportunity for us to ponder on the different ways in which men and women face death.

The fabric of Webster's verse is densely woven. The large number of critical articles on different aspects of the imagery of *The Duchess of Malfi* testifies to the impossibility of his meaning being fully apprehended by a single experience of the play, whether in the theatre or the study.[18] Like Shakespeare's, his images are not inert,[19] but are reflected in action.[20] Some, indeed, are based on the combined impact of picture and verse in Renaissance emblem books.[21] In 1970, Inga-Stina Ewbank considered Webster's dramatic art in terms of Renaissance perspective painting.[22] More recently, his use of an emblematic technique has been studied.[23]

Webster's themes and images are inseparable from his sources, upon which R.W. Dent's impressive study *John Webster's Borrowing* sheds necessary light. Knowledge of the extent to which Webster's verse is

---

[18] Analyses of other aspects of theme and imagery may be found in G. Wilson Knight, '*The Duchess of Malfi*', *MRev* 4 (1967), 88–113; Leslie Duer, 'The Landscape of Imagination in *The Duchess of Malfi*', *MLS* 10, no. 1 (Winter, 1979–80), reprinted in *John Webster's 'The Duchess of Malfi*', edited by Harold Bloom (New York, New Haven and Philadelphia, 1987), pp. 31–39; Paula S. Berggren, 'Spatial Imagery in Webster's Tragedies', *SEL* 20 (1980), 287–303; Anat Feinberg, 'Observation and Theatricality in Webster's *The Duchess of Malfi*', *TRI* 6 (1981), 36–44.

[19] See John Reibetanz, *The 'Lear' World: A Study of 'King Lear' in its Dramatic Context* (Toronto and Buffalo: University of Toronto Press, 1977) which, in method and content, is parallel to similar analyses of Webster's work: e.g. Lee Bliss, *The World's Perspective: John Webster and the Jacobean Drama* (Brighton: The Harvester Press, 1983).

[20] Schuman, 'The Ring and the Jewel'; Rebhorn, 'Circle, Sword and the Futile Quest'; Marion Lomax, *Stage Images and Traditions: Shakespeare to Ford* (London, 1987).

[21] See S. Schuman, 'Two Notes upon Emblems and the English Renaissance Drama', *N&Q* n.s. 18 (1971), 28–29; R. E. R. Madelaine, '*The Duchess of Malfi* and Two Emblems in Whitney and Peacham', *N&Q* n.s. 29 (1982), 146–47.

[22] 'Webster's Realism, or "A Cunning Piece Wrought Perspective"', in *John Webster*, edited by Morris, pp. 157–78

[23] See Catherine Belsey, 'Emblem and Antithesis in *The Duchess of Malfi*', *RenD* n.s. 11 (1980), pp. 115–34; Kathleen McLuskie, 'Drama and Sexual Politics: The Case of Webster's Duchess', *TD* 7 (1985), pp. 77–91.

indebted to or plays variations on other men's ideas and phrases allows us to appreciate what kind of mind he had and gives an added resonance to the speeches through which his characters live. We do not go to the theatre to spot Webster's sources, but we may profit from an understanding of which authors most influenced him.[24]

Webster's imagery is just as closely bound to his dramatic structure. One response to the allegation of structural incoherence in *The Duchess of Malfi* lies in an examination of the play's structural rhythm: an approach first made by Inga-Stina Ekeblad in 1957 and developed by Christina Luckyj in 1989.[25] Another lies in a study of its unifying themes.[26] Yet the feeling has persisted that Webster's world – expressed through structure and image – is one of chaos and nightmare. Thus Wayne A. Rebhorn has written of 'Circle, Sword and the Futile Quest: The Nightmare World of Webster's *Duchess of Malfi*',[27] and Lois Potter of 'Realism versus Nightmare: Problems of Staging *The Duchess of Malfi*'.[28]

In both theatre and study one is made aware of this nightmare quality by Webster's juxtaposition of opposites in theme – appearance and reality; light and dark; love and death – and in character. In 1964 Jane Marie Luecke, OSB, saw these as elements which confused the tragic effect of the play.[29] More recent critics – most notably, Jacqueline Pearson and Lee Bliss – have given Webster greater credit for knowing what he was about and for being in sympathy with the dramatic experiments of his contemporaries.[30]

In Jacobean cast lists, as in life, the men took precedence, but it is surprising to find Bosola's name at the top. In the play, he is introduced to us before either of the Aragonian brothers, and in critical analyses he often commands more attention that the Duchess herself: a fact which

---

[24] See also O. Brückl, 'Sir Philip Sidney's *Arcadia* as a Source for John Webster's *The Duchess of Malfi*', *ESA* 8 (1965), 31–55; David L. Frost, *The School of Shakespeare: The Influence of Shakespeare on English Drama 1600–1642* (Cambridge, 1968), pp. 145–54.

[25] Inga-Stina Ekeblad, 'Webster's Constructional Rhythm', *ELH* 24 (1957), 165–76; Luckyj, *A Winter's Snake*.

[26] See William E. Mahaney, *Deception in the John Webster Plays: An Analytical Study*, Jacobean Drama Studies (Salzburg, 1973), pp. 164–79.

[27] See n. 16, above.

[28] In *The Triple Bond: Plays, mainly Shakespearean, in Performance*, edited by Joseph G. Price (University Park and London: Pennsylvania State University Press, 1975), pp. 170–89.

[29] '*The Duchess of Malfi*: Comic and Satiric Confusion in a Tragedy', *SEL* 4 (1964), 275–90.

[30] See J.R. Mulryne, 'Webster and the Uses of Tragicomedy' in *John Webster*, edited by Morris, pp. 131–55; Jacqueline Pearson, *Tragedy and Tragicomedy in the Plays of John Webster* (Manchester, 1980); Bliss, *The World's Perspective*.

the length of his part, his 'continuous contact with the audience'[31] and his *contemptus mundi* stance make, perhaps, unsurprising,[32] though Lee Bliss neatly characterizes him as lacking 'the courage of his own aphorisms'.[33]

PERSPECTIVES ON WEBSTER'S DUCHESS

The most important difference between Webster's drama and prose accounts of the Duchess's life is his refusal to make judgemental statements about her. Though Antonio's praise of her in Act I, Scene i underlines her purity and piety, these qualities are questioned by others because she lives in a court which is both corrupt and corrupting. They are questioned by Webster's audience, too, and recent critics have not failed to assess her comparative guilt or innocence. Some find her guilty, but deserving of compassion.[34] R.F. Whitman comments that 'while it might be far-fetched to associate the Duchess, rather than Ferdinand, with the "curs'd example" that spreads poison through "the whole land" ... it seems mere romantic infatuation with her acknowledged charms to free her of substantial responsibility for what happens, or to claim her as a model of "goodness".'[35] For Joyce E. Peterson, however, there is no doubt that the Duchess *is* the 'curs'd example' whence the ills of her commonweal flow.[36] Defenders of the Duchess stress her integrity, which Susan C. Baker finds is maintained, not only in her marriage, but after her initial defiance of her brothers,[37] while Kathleen McLuskie remarks on the Duchess's wit and independence in this defiance.[38]

---

[31] McLuskie and Uglow, p. 8

[32] See Louis D. Giannetti, 'A Contemporary View of *The Duchess of Malfi*', *CompD* 3 (1969–70), 297–307, who describes Bosola as 'the only character in the play who can develop' (p. 300); David Luisi, 'The Function of Bosola in *The Duchess of Malfi*', *ES* 53 (1972), 509–13; S.W. Sullivan, 'The Tendency to Rationalize in *The White Devil* and *The Duchess of Malfi*', *YES* 4 (1974), 77–84; Bettie Anne Doebler, 'Continuity in the Art of Dying: *The Duchess of Malfi*', *CompD* 14 (1980), 203–15.

[33] *The World's Perspective*, p. 139

[34] See P.F. Vernon, 'The Duchess of Malfi's Guilt', *N&Q* n.s. 10 (1963), 335–38; W.W.G. Dwyer, *A Study of John Webster's Use of Renaissance Natural and Moral Philosophy*, Jacobean Drama Studies (Salzburg, 1973), p. 58.

[35] 'The Moral Paradox of Webster's Tragedy', *PMLA* 90 (1975), 894–903 (p. 897)

[36] *Curs'd Example: 'The Duchess of Malfi' and Commonweal Tragedy* (Columbia and London: University of Columbia Press, 1978)

[37] In *TSLL* 22 (1980), 343–57; see also Joan M. Lord, '*The Duchess of Malfi*: "the Spirit of Greatness" and "of Woman"', *SEL* 16 (1976), 305–17.

[38] 'Drama and Sexual Politics', p. 79

The Duchess of Malfi has received considerable attention from feminine and feminist critics, whose work often points to the difficulty of assessing the impact of a character as complex as Webster's heroine.[39] Being both historical and fictional, she conforms to and suffers as the Renaissance stereotype of a lusty widow.[40] It is, moreover, for an accumulation of wrongdoings that the Duchess undergoes torture and death. The view taken of her by her brothers, her subjects and, initially, by Bosola reflects the prejudices of seventeenth-century society. Webster, however, presents her situation in a way that poses questions about the prejudice, weakness or perversity of the men with whom she has to deal.

Early in the play her brother Ferdinand exclaims:

> Marry? they are most luxurious,
> Will wed twice.   (I.ii.218–19)

A romantic interpretation sees the Duchess as 'in love with' Antonio, but her courtship of him, immediately after she has denied to her brothers any intention of marrying, could be interpreted as a manifestation of unseemly boldness and lust as well as deviousness. Antonio, who had previously idealized her as a model of chaste behaviour, is obviously surprised by her passion, no less than by her proposal of marriage. He is beneath her in social rank, and their union thus imperils her family's honour, if not the inheritance of the young Duke of Amalfi.[41] In so far as her marriage is secret, the Duchess's pregnancies proclaim her lust, and the common people, as Antonio reports,

> do directly say
> She is a strumpet.   (III.i.25–26)

Hostile observers – who include some modern critics – have grounds for coarse interpretation of the Duchess's actions, considering that she is guilty of pursuing private pleasure at the expense of the public weal. As an historical figure she improved the economy of Amalfi; in the world of the play she is accused of wasting money on expensive court entertainments. Presenting the Duchess in intimate close-up within the confines of a court where her perverse and dangerously obsessive brothers hold sway and a society that is male-dominated and prejudiced, Webster shifts perspectives to allow us to see the contrasts between

[39] See Lisa Jardine, *Still Harping on Daughters*; Catherine Belsey, *The Subject of Tragedy: Identity and Difference in Renaissance Drama* (London and New York: Methuen, 1985); Kathleen McLuskie, *Renaissance Dramatists*, Feminist Readings (Hemel Hempstead: Harvester Wheatsheaf, 1989); Dympna Callaghan, *Women and Gender in Renaissance Tragedy: A Study of King Lear, Othello, The Duchess of Malfi and The White Devil* (Hemel Hempstead: Harvester Wheatsheaf, 1989).

[40] See Jardine, *Still Harping on Daughters*, pp. 68–98.

[41] Ibid.

internal and external views of his heroine; between the stereotype and the individual; between the subject of a madman's torture and the witty and brave lover, wife and mother which her stage actions reveal her to be.

After he has privately received intelligence that she has borne a child – presumably out of wedlock – Ferdinand publicly proposes that his sister marry the great Count Malateste. Her brother the Cardinal, who had ecclesiastical authority to forbid any priest in his diocese to marry the Duchess, warns her against marrying secretly. In English law, her contract with Antonio was legal; and its consummation made it binding.[42] Whatever the original audience believed or thought about the remarriage of widows – regal or otherwise – in the world of the play the Duchess could expect no less than punishment for succumbing to the fearful madness which Cariola saw as related either to the spirit of greatness or of woman. Cariola owed her much of pity, and her compassionate impulse, later to touch even Bosola, should also touch the audience. Lisa Jardine has summarized the situation thus:

> Whatever is to be discovered by considering women figures in literature, it is unlikely to be a simple matter to read it out of the text of novel or play. However much of an inspiration the Duchess may appear to us – the strong woman challenging conventional attitudes – she is not a 'real' woman, neither is she a direct reflection of individual women of her time. She is a transposition of a complex of attitudes towards women into a 'travesty' ... of seventeenth-century womanhood. The strength we enjoy in performance is her actual weakness – perhaps that is what makes the Duchess of Malfi so captivating and poignant a stage figure.[43]

To this attractive and persuasive argument I would add another dimension. Though she is neither the alabaster figure kneeling at her husband's tomb, nor an idealized plaster saint – she is accused of jesting with religion, and calls the cautious Cariola a superstitious fool – the Duchess does seem concerned to live and die like a Christian, as well as a prince.

Between the evidence of her apparent lustfulness and her suffering punishment for it we are allowed an insight into her fruitful marriage. Pregnancy may indeed have been, for Renaissance man, an image of female sexuality, but both the Psalms of David (Psalm 127.5) and the Anglican marriage service recognized children as a blessing from God. Though married outside the Church, the Duchess creates for Antonio and herself a ritual which acknowledges the needs for which Christian

---

[42] See Additional Notes, pp. 134–35 below.

[43] 'The Duchess of Malfi: A Case Study in the Literary Representation of Women', in Teaching the Text, edited by Susanne Kappeler and Norman Bryson (London, 1983), p. 216

marriage was, according to the Book of Common Prayer, ordained. In the domestic world of Act III, Scene ii, she discusses the possibility of her brothers becoming godparents to future children, and her previously shy husband speaks eloquently to Cariola of the joys of marriage. Rank and its concomitant *savoir faire* force the Duchess to woo Antonio, to accuse him falsely and to plan for their flight, but the loquacity which may be seen as unseemly boldness becomes an amusement to Antonio and Cariola even if their joke turns sour, with the unexpected arrival of Ferdinand. The absence of the young Duke of Amalfi has been remarked by critics. It is perhaps more surprising that Antonio's three children are present, and their innocent existence is emphasized by their parents' care for them. If they lack the eloquent precocity of young Giovanni of *The White Devil* or the Princes in the Tower as characterized by Shakespeare in *Richard III* (Act III, Scene i), their silent lives and deaths surely invoke some of the pity felt at the loss of Macduff's pretty ones (Shakespeare, *Macbeth* Act IV, Scene ii; Scene iii, ll. 204–27). In heroic terms, the Duchess defies the evil in her court and her brothers' hearts; in Christian terms, she makes a good end.

Different members of the audience and different generations of theatre-goers bring their own experience of life to bear on the Duchess's situation, making an imaginative leap to understand why John Webster chose to recreate and reinterpret this historical figure for his contemporaries in a way that is still valid for us. As readers we may find her guilty; as theatre-goers we must respond to the living actor and his interpretation.

EARLY PERFORMANCES OF WEBSTER'S PLAYS

Caesar's Fall and *Lady Jane* were written for the Admiral's Men and the Earl of Worcester's Men respectively. The city comedies *Westward Ho!* and *Northward Ho!* were written by Dekker and Webster for the company of Paul's Boys, who performed them in their private theatre. Upon the accession of James I, the Earl of Worcester's Men changed their name to Queen Anne's Servants. Under their alternative style of the Queen's Men they performed *The White Devil*, *The Devil's Law-Case* and *Keep the Widow Waking* at the Red Bull, their theatre in Clerkenwell. The King's Men presented *Anything for a Quiet Life* at the Blackfriars in 1621.

STAGING 'THE DUCHESS OF MALFI'

Webster created *The Duchess of Malfi* with Shakespeare's company, the King's Men, in mind.[44] It was acted at the Blackfriars and their public house, the Globe, between 1612 and 1614. At this time the company was both prestigious and financially secure. More importantly, the personnel of the company, which comprised twelve adult actors, changed little between 1608 and 1642, thus allowing the development of great skill in ensemble playing. Having at first been unable to use the Blackfriars theatre, which they had bought in 1596, by 1610 they had established it as their winter home, whence they transferred – probably in April – for a summer season at the Globe. In the Induction which he had written for Marston's *Malcontent* Webster presented the three leading actors – Burbage, Lowin and Condell, well-known to the audiences of the Globe – as themselves.

The double cast-list of Q1 indicates that the play was revived at least once, and possibly twice, between its first performance and publication in 1623.[45] Bosola heads the list, thus taking precedence over Ferdinand; John Lowin's part over Richard Burbage's. At this time Lowin, a thick-set man, was about thirty-seven, a highly-experienced actor who had been Shakespeare's Falstaff and Henry VIII and had taken leading roles in Jonson's plays. Richard Burbage, who had been Shakespeare's Richard III, Hamlet, King Lear and Othello, was in his mid-forties, a renowned tragedian whose casting indicates the extent to which Webster wished to differentiate Ferdinand's character from that of the less tragic Cardinal. Burbage's previous portrayal of Othello might, indeed, have provided the audience with visible indications of Ferdinand's incestuous jealousy of the Duchess. After Burbage's death, in 1619, Joseph Taylor, an experienced actor who had worked with Prince Charles's Men and Lady Elizabeth's Men, succeeded to this and other of Burbage's leading roles. Henry Condell, more famous as responsible – with John Hem-inges – for the publication of the First Folio of Shakespeare than as an actor, was the first Cardinal. When he retired, in 1619, the part was taken over by Richard Robinson, who had earlier been renowned as a boy actress. He performed in *Catiline* and Jonson showed his appreciation of the skill of Dick Robinson in *The Devil is an Ass*, Act II, Scene iii. Although Richard Sharpe is assigned to the part of the Duchess, he was probably too young to have created the part, which could well have been played by Robinson before 1619, and by Sharpe thereafter.

---

[44] See Brown, pp. xvii-xxiv; Keith Sturgess, *Jacobean Private Theatre*, Theatre Production Studies (London and New York: Routledge & Kegan Paul, 1987), especially Chapter 6: '"A Perspective that shows us Hell": *The Duchess of Malfi* at the Blackfriars', pp. 97–122.

[45] See p. xvi above and pp. 2–3 below.

Similarly, John Rice was probably too young to have played Pescaro in the original production, and John Thompson, assigned to Julia, was not known as a boy actress before 1621. Thomas Pollard may not have been in the company in 1612–14, to have taken Silvio's part then. Nine years of age in September 1614, Robert Pallant might have managed Cariola's part, but hardly that of the doctor. J.R. Brown suggests that he may have taken both parts in a revival, when he was sixteen or seventeen.[46]

As young boys, William Ostler and John Underwood, the creators of Antonio and Delio, had both belonged to the Children of the Chapel and thus had experience of private theatre drama and acting conditions before working in the Blackfriars. After Ostler's death, in 1614, he was succeeded in Antonio's part by Robert Benfield, who later developed into a leading tragedian.

Writing from London on 7 February 1618, Orazio Busino, the Venetian envoy, described a performance which we assume he had seen recently. Though he confused the Duchess and Julia, stating that the Cardinal was shown giving poison to one of his sisters in a question of honour, Busino gave an account of a procession organized by the Cardinal, who pretended to make a prayer before an altar erected on stage; he also described Act III, Scene iv and deplored the fact that the Cardinal was produced 'in public, with a harlot on his knee.'[47]

Though performed at both theatres occupied by the King's Men, *The Duchess of Malfi* lent itself rather to performance in the Blackfriars, an enclosed hall which seated 600–700 spectators, of whom a few sat on the stage and the majority in the pit or galleries. Scholars disagree on the effects which might have been achieved by darkening the auditorium and illuminating the stage by torches and candles,[48] but we may be certain that the small stage allowed the actors to achieve greater naturalism and greater intimacy than was possible in the large amphitheatre of the Globe, which accommodated over 2,000 spectators on three sides of a stage twice the size of that in the Blackfriars. The whispering that characterizes court intrigue, and of which the Duchess complains in IV.ii.218–19, well suited the ambience of the Blackfriars. Another factor contributing to the Blackfriars ambience was the division of plays into acts. From the practical point of view, these pauses allowed the candles to be trimmed. More notably, they were marked by the performance of music. The music for the Madmen's Song in Act IV, Scene ii, composed

---

[46] See Brown, p. xxi.

[47] See *John Webster*, edited by G.K. and S.K. Hunter, Penguin Critical Anthologies (Harmondsworth, 1969), pp. 31–2; Sturgess, *Jacobean Private Theatre*, pp. 109–12; McLuskie and Uglow, pp. 4–5, 109, 141.

[48] See R.B. Graves, '*The Duchess of Malfi* at the Globe and Blackfriars', *RenD* n.s. 9 (1978), 193–209; Alan C. Dessen, *Elizabethan Stage Conventions and Modern Interpreters* (Cambridge: Cambridge University Press, 1984); Sturgess, *Jacobean Private Theatre*, p. 46.

by Robert Johnson, has survived and is printed as Appendix II in J.R. Brown's edition of the play.

The Duchess of Malfi opens with the intimate conversation between two old friends, and though the stage quickly fills to create a court scene, within that scene – as elsewhere in the drama – characters form into groups to whom the audience's attention is directed as if by a camera, in close-up.[49] As Inga-Stina Ekeblad has shown, the characteristic movement of a central Webster scene is one 'from swift, foreboding, dialogue to slowly analyzing speeches, practically monologues'.[50] Though the Duchess never soliloquizes, this is a tragedy of intimate exchanges and monologues which are often delivered in (stage) darkness. It is also characterized by silent movement, epitomized most chillingly in Ferdinand's

> Strangling is a very quiet death. (V.iv.33)

The 1623 title-page declares that the text contains divers things that the length of the play would not bear in the presentment, but we do not know which scenes or lines were cut. The play is longer than most printed in quarto. Keith Sturgess calculates that it is about a fifth longer than the average Globe play and probably two-fifths longer than the average Blackfriars play.[51] Nevertheless, *The Duchess of Malfi*, with 2,864 lines of speech, is shorter than many of Shakespeare's plays, among which seven have over 3,500 lines.[52] The 1989/90 RSC production had a three-hour performance time, and a single fifteen-minute interval.

On 26 December 1630, Charles I attended a performance of *The Duchess of Malfi* which the King's Men put on at the Cockpit Theatre, Whitehall, that winter. After the Restoration the play was in the repertoire of the Duke's Company, becoming one of their best stock tragedies. In 1707 an altered version – *The Unfortunate Dutchess of Malfy or the Unnatural Brothers* – was produced at the Queen's Theatre in the Haymarket. The printed text (Q4) is not only cut itself, but contains printed indications of where further cuts were made in performance.[53] Adherence to eighteenth-century concepts of decorum dictated the removal of as much sexual passion as possible, together with much of Webster's sententiousness. The casting of Barton Booth, the company's

---

[49] See Sturgess, *Jacobean Private Theatre*, pp. 105–7. His suggestion that one way of concentrating attention on individual commentators is to freeze the action of those whom they anatomize was realized in the 1989/90 RSC production.

[50] 'Webster's Constructional Rhythm', p. 175

[51] *Jacobean Private Theatre*, pp. 103–4

[52] i.e. *Hamlet*, *Richard III*, *Coriolanus*, *Cymbeline*, *Othello*, *Antony and Cleopatra*, *Troilus and Cressida*

[53] See Note on the Text, p. xxxix below.

chief actor, as Antonio indicates a shift in tragic emphasis which this truncated version supported.[54]

Lewis Theobald's adaptation, *The Fatal Secret: A Tragedy*, published in 1735, was staged at the Theatre Royal, Covent Garden, in April 1733. Its action is confined to Malfi and limited to the day on which the Duchess and Antonio have been secretly married, off-stage. Julia is removed, but the creation of Ferdinand's secretary – to perform some of Bosola's darker deeds – allows the latter to preserve the heroine's life. After her brothers' deaths, the Duchess is happily reunited not only with Antonio, but with her twelve-year-old son, the young Duke.[55]

Julia is also absent from R.H. Horne's version of the play, first put on by Samuel Phelps's company at Sadler's Wells, in 1850, starring Isabella Glyn as the Duchess. Then, and later, it proved to be the most popular of the non-Shakespearean plays in Phelps's Elizabethan and Jacobean repertoire. In October 1892, William Poel directed two performances of a new version of the play at the Opéra Comique. Julia was still absent, but Poel's production anticipated twentieth-century attempts to locate the play in a Renaissance context and placed more reliance on Webster's original text.[56]

In 1919, at the Lyric Theatre, Hammersmith, in two Sunday performances given under the auspices of the Phoenix Society, Julia returned in the person of Edith Evans, while Cathleen Nesbitt played the Duchess. Julia disappeared again in 1922, in Nugent Monck's production at the Maddermarket Theatre, Norwich, and was also absent when the play was staged at the Embassy Theatre, Swiss Cottage, in 1935.

George Rylands, who had been a pupil of F.L. Lucas, of King's College, Cambridge, the distinguished editor of Webster, worked on four productions of *The Duchess of Malfi* between 1924 and 1946, combining both scholarly and dramatic interests in the play. He had himself taken the part of the Duchess in an undergraduate performance and was asked to direct one of the most famous of twentieth-century productions, at the Haymarket Theatre, in 1945, with John Gielgud playing Ferdinand and Peggy Ashcroft the Duchess.[57]

Peggy Ashcroft, who said the part of the Duchess was her favourite, portrayed her again, for the Stratford-on-Avon Company in 1960, when Eric Porter was Ferdinand and Patrick Wymark played Bosola. Since then, a succession of distinguished actresses have interpreted Webster's Duchess on the English stage: Judy Parfitt and Judi Dench (1971), Jane Lapotaire (1976), Janet Suzman (1979), Helen Mirren (1980), Eleanor

---

[54] McLuskie and Uglow, pp. 18–20
[55] McLuskie and Uglow, pp. 20–23
[56] McLuskie and Uglow, pp. 24–35; Brown, pp. lvi–lvii
[57] McLuskie and Uglow, pp. 35–43; Brown, pp. lvii–lix

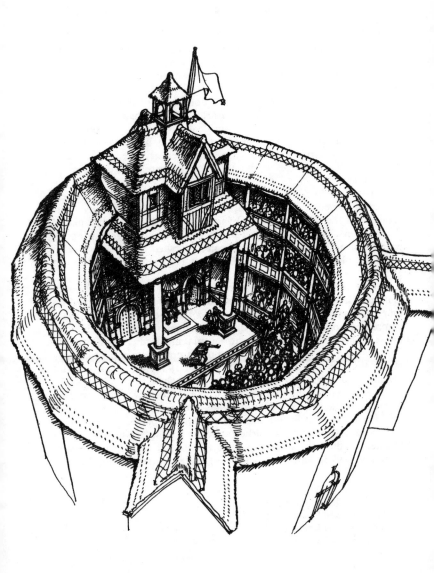

Bron (1985), and Harriet Walter (1989). She is not, however, the romantic heroine realized in the nineteenth century. Strong casting has restored the importance of Bosola to a balanced view of the tragedy – Richard Pasco (1971), Bob Hoskins (1980), Ian McKellan (1985) – while Michael Williams (1971), Mike Gwilym (1980) and Jonathan Hyde (1985) have portrayed Ferdinand.[58]

Commenting on productions of both *The White Devil* and *The Duchess of Malfi*, Richard Allen Cave reminds us:

> Webster could discern the spirit ... the inner dimension of self that keeps pace with a character's progress through the physical realities of plot and that finally in death gains total possession of the character's consciousness. The challenge for a director and cast is to keep an audience attuned to that other dimension of being which is best achieved by exploring the dramatic possibilities of the verse.[59]

The interest of touring and experimental companies in the play and the range and type of theatre in which it has been presented have combined to allow twentieth-century audiences, no less than Webster's own, to experience the effect of Webster's tragedy in different types of performance space, with a range of costume, settings and props. Whether performed publicly, in a large, subsidized theatre, or privately, by a small group of students, *The Duchess of Malfi* still generates tension, arouses emotion and communicates through poetry.

[58] For accounts of other productions see Brown, pp. lxvi–lix; David Carnegie, 'A Preliminary Checklist of Productions of the Plays of John Webster', *RORD* 26 (1983), 55–63; Richard Allen Cave, '*The White Devil*' and '*The Duchess of Malfi*', Text and Performance (Basingstoke and London: Macmillan Education, 1988); Luckyj, *A Winter's Snake*; McLuskie and Uglow, pp. 24–62. *RORD* publishes frequent accounts of productions of Renaissance drama. Where relevant, references to productions between 1960 and 1990 are included in the notes on the text.

[59] '*The White Devil*' and '*The Duchess of Malfi*', p. 70

NOTE ON THE TEXT

This edition of *The Duchess of Malfi* is based on the text of the first quarto (BL copies 644.f.72 and Ashley 2207). This has been collated with the three later quartos and principal modern editions, and emended where necessary. Q1 (1623) is the only authoritative text. Previous scholars' collation of several copies has revealed the existence of an uncorrected and two corrected states, which I have designated Q1a, Q1b and Q1c. The second corrected state, Q1c, is found only in sheet G, outer forme: in this edition III.ii.110–40, 201–73; III.iii.2–31. Where press variants are clearly alterations rather than corrections – e.g. the change from 'pewterers' to 'painters' at III.iii.19 and changes in the directions for the ceremony of the Cardinal's instalment in the habit of a soldier, in III.iv – we can deduce that they are authorial. Further proof of Webster's presence in the printing-house may be found in the fact that stage directions have been added to text already prepared for printing by the expedients of placing them in the margins – e.g. III.ii.71 s.d., 150 s.d.; IV.i.143 s.d. – or crowding the speeches together.

As J.R. Brown has demonstrated,[1] Q1 was set up by two compositors, working from a manuscript that had probably been copied out by Ralph Crane, a professional scribe associated with the King's Men. Compositor A followed his copy closely and, in order to reproduce the large number of colons and semicolons which are typical of Crane's usage, often took more than his fair share of the available supply of these. Consequently, Compositor B had to substitute commas for some of the colons and semicolons in his stint of the work. The punctuation of this edition is based on Compositor A's practice, and an attempt has been made to make passages set by Compositor B correspond to this. Some idiosyncrasies and ambiguities of the Q1 punctuation – frequent capitalization, the use of colons for stops, the placing of commas between subject and verb, the use of brackets for phrases in parenthesis – have been removed where their inclusion would prove a distraction to modern readers. Where appropriate, Q1's question marks have been silently changed to exclamation marks, and noted in the collation where there is any doubt in the matter. Interrupted speeches – indicated in Q1 by commas or colons – are marked by dashes. Nevertheless, the number of exclamation marks and dashes introduced into the text has been kept to a minimum.

Q1 title-page claims that the copy is 'perfect and exact', printing divers things 'that the length of the play would not beare in the Presentment'.

---

[1] See J.R. Brown, 'The Printing of John Webster's Plays (II)', *SB* 8 (1956), 117–20.

Written by a dramatist who derived both general and particular stimulus
from other men's words and phrases, Q1 was published with the reader
rather than the actor in mind. The reader's attention was directed to
the play's many sententiae by quotation marks and/or the use of italics.
In this edition italics are used throughout. Similarly, Q1 contains 'block
entries' – i.e. lists at the beginning of each scene of all characters to
appear therein – and is singularly lacking in stage directions. In line
with modern editorial practice, I have substituted precise indications of
characters' entrances and exits and provided directions to allow the
reader to envisage stage action. All Q1's stage directions, other than
'block entries', are incorporated in the text. The collation notes if they
were originally printed in the margin, since, as Brown has argued, this
suggests Webster's careful overseeing of the printers' work.[2] Speech
prefixes, abbreviated and in italic script in Qq, have been expanded. All
editorial additions to text and stage directions are indicated by square
brackets. In accordance with the style of the New Mermaids, editorial
stage directions are unpointed. Act and Scene divisions, given in full
and in Latin in Q1, are here marked by Roman numerals.

The spelling of the Q1 text has been modernized, but some older
forms of words – e.g. lanthorn – have been allowed to stand. Where two
or more spellings occur – e.g. *ore* and *o'er*; *–de* and *–'d*; *taine*, *ta'en* and
tane – the commonest has been used throughout: i.e. *o'er*; *–'d* and *tane*.

Q2 (1640), based on Q1, introduces both minor emendation and
minor errors. Q3 (1678), derived from Q2, corrects some errors and
introduces others. Q4 is an abbreviated and altered version of the play,
published in 1708 as *The Unfortunate Dutchess of Malfy or the Unnatural
Brothers*.[3] The whole of Act III, Scene iv is omitted; many speeches are
cut or rephrased so that there is more emphasis on the play's political
and less on its sexual concerns. In addition, many passages are marked
for extra cutting in performance. Where the text does follow that of
previous quartos it is based on Q3, with emendations made by reference
to Q1. Q4 also has some sensible corrections of errors in all three
previous quartos: see, for example, the collation of II.i.124, 131; II.ii.79,
90; IV.i.89. On the other hand, the printer was sometimes baffled by
variation in earlier quartos. A turned *n* in Q1 at II.ii.1 reproduced
'teatchines' (i.e. tetchiness) as 'teatchiues'. The substitution of 'v' for
the apparent 'u' made this 'teatchives' in Qq2–3. Q4 reads 'eager'. Q4
is interesting as an example of the shaping influence of early eighteenth-
century taste. Moreover, its generally useful additions to the stage
directions call the scholar's attention to the play's active life in the
theatre.

---

[2] See Brown, pp. lxiii–lxv.
[3] A detailed, though not entirely accurate account of Q4 as a play text for the
1707 production at the Queen's Theatre is given by McLuskie and Uglow.

This edition does not give a complete collation of the quartos. Except where changes provide interesting information about the transmission of the text between 1623 and 1708, only those variants which alter or emend the Q1 text are considered. Turned letters, obvious minor typographical errors and variations in orthography are not included.

NOTE ON THE REVISED EDITION (1993)

The Duchess of Malfi was first published in the New Mermaids a few months before J.R. Brown's text for The Revels Plays series. It has therefore been collated throughout with Brown's text as well as that of D.C. Gunby in *John Webster: Three Plays* (Penguin English Library, 1972). The readings of those editions have not, however, been incorporated in the Textual Appendix.

Though the Introduction and notes have been extensively revised, the text presented here – with the exception of the identification of the madmen in IV.ii – is substantially as it was printed in 1964. At I.ii.30 I have incorporated in the text my earlier conjecture that Q1 'Ismael' should read 'Israel'; and at I.ii.36 I have accepted that the line belongs to Ferdinand. At I.ii.116 'your' has been altered to 'you' and at I.ii.404 I have accepted Brown's reading of 'bind'. In II.i.33 McIlwraith and Brown's reading is accepted and at l. 35 'plaster' has replaced the usual 'plastic'. In II.i a missing question mark has been restored to l. 87 and in III.ii.150 a stage direction has been repositioned. In IV.i I have substituted 'child' for 'children' in l. 55 s.d. and 'vapours' for 'vipers' in l. 90. In IV.ii a missing stage direction has been supplied in l. 230 and in V.v brackets in l. 51 s.d. have been repositioned.

FURTHER READING

Books and articles which throw light on particular passages of the play are listed in the notes on the text. The following is a select chronological bibliography of works which have made valuable contributions to the study of John Webster and *The Duchess of Malfi*.

Charles Lamb, *Specimens of English Dramatic Poets, who lived about the Time of Shakespeare: with notes* (London, 1808)

Edgar Elmer Stoll, *John Webster: The Periods of his Work as Determined by His Relations to the Drama of His Day* (Boston, MA, 1905)

Rupert Brooke, *John Webster and the Elizabethan Drama* (London: Sidgwick & Jackson, 1916)

Peter Haworth, *English Hymns and Ballads and Other Studies in Popular Literature* (Oxford, 1927)

M.C. Bradbrook, *Themes and Conventions of Elizabethan Tragedy* (Cambridge and London: Cambridge University Press, 1935; 2nd edn, 1980)

Moody E. Prior, *The Language of Tragedy* (New York, 1947)

Clifford Leech, *John Webster: A Critical Study* (London, 1951)

Gabriele Baldini, *John Webster e il Linguaggio della Tragedia* (Rome, 1953)

John Russell Brown, 'The Printing of John Webster's Plays', 3 parts, *SB* 6 (1954), 117–40; 8 (1956), 113–28; 15 (1962), 57–69

Travis Bogard, *The Tragic Satire of John Webster* (Berkeley and Los Angeles: University of California Press, 1955)

Hereward T. Price, 'The Function of Imagery in Webster', *PMLA* 70 (1955), 717–39

J.R. Mulryne, '*The White Devil* and *The Duchess of Malfi*', in *Jacobean Theatre*, edited by John Russell Brown and Bernard Harris, *SUAS* 1 (1960), pp. 201–25

R.W. Dent, *John Webster's Borrowing* (Berkeley and Los Angeles: University of California Press, 1960)

Gunnar Boklund, '*The Duchess of Malfi*': *Sources, Themes, Characters* (Cambridge, MA: Harvard University Press, 1962)

J.L. Calderwood, '*The Duchess of Malfi*: Styles of Ceremony', *EIC* 12 (1962), 133–47

Clifford Leech, *John Webster: 'The Duchess of Malfi'*, Studies in English Literature, 8 (London: Edward Arnold, 1963)

J.G. Riewald, 'Shakespeare Burlesque in John Webster's *The Duchess of Malfi*' in *English Studies Presented to R.W. Zandvoort* (Amsterdam, 1964), pp. 172–89

Fernand Lagarde, *John Webster*, 2 vols (Toulouse, 1968)

Peter B. Murray, *A Study of John Webster* (The Hague and Paris: Mouton, 1969)

John Webster: A Critical Anthology, edited by G.K. and S.K. Hunter, Penguin Critical Anthologies (Harmondsworth, 1969)

John Webster, edited by Brian Morris, Mermaid Critical Commentaries (London: Ernest Benn, 1970)

J.W. Lever, *The Tragedy of State* (London: Methuen, 1971)

Ralph Berry, *The Art of John Webster* (Oxford: The Clarendon Press, 1972)

S.W. Sullivan, 'The Tendency to Rationalize in *The White Devil* and *The Duchess of Malfi*', *YES* 4 (1974), 77–84

Lois Potter, 'Realism versus Nightmare: Problems of Staging *The Duchess of Malfi*' in *The Triple Bond: Plays, mainly Shakespearean, in Performance*, edited by Joseph G. Price (University Park and London: Pennsylvania State University Press, 1975), pp. 170–89

Mary Edmond, 'In Search of John Webster', *TLS*, 24 December 1976, pp. 1621–22

R.B. Graves, '*The Duchess of Malfi* at the Globe and Blackfriars', *RenD* n. s. 9 (1978), 193–209

Joyce E. Peterson, *Curs'd Example: 'The Duchess of Malfi' and Commonweal Tragedy* (Columbia, MO, and London: University of Missouri Press, 1978)

Nicholas Brooke, *Horrid Laughter in Jacobean Tragedy* (London: Open Books, 1979)

Catherine Belsey, 'Emblem and Antithesis in *The Duchess of Malfi*', *RenD* n.s. 11 (1980), 115–34

M.C. Bradbrook, *John Webster: Citizen and Dramatist* (London: Weidenfeld and Nicolson, 1980)

Jacqueline Pearson, *Tragedy and Tragicomedy in the Plays of John Webster* (Manchester: Manchester University Press, 1980)

Lee Bliss, *The World's Perspective: John Webster and the Jacobean Drama* (New Brunswick, NJ: Rutgers University Press and Brighton: The Harvester Press, 1983)

Lisa Jardine, *Still Harping on Daughters: Women and Drama in the Age of Shakespeare* (Hassocks: The Harvester Press, 1983; 2nd edn, New York, London, etc.: Harvester Wheatsheaf, 1989)

Charles R. Forker, *Skull Beneath the Skin: The Achievement of John Webster* (Carbondale and Edwardsville: Southern Illinois University Press, 1986)

Richard Allen Cave, '*The White Devil*' and '*The Duchess of Malfi*', Text and Performance (Basingstoke and London: Macmillan Education, 1988)

5–6 *priuatly, at the Black-Friers; and publiquely at the Globe* i.e. the play was performed in both the theatres owned by the King's Men, which differed in size, construction and stage conditions. See Introduction, pp. xxxii–xxxiii.

8 *The perfect and exact Coppy* not a claim to be taken literally. See J.R. Brown, 'The Printing of John Webster's Plays (I)', *SB* 6 (1954), 117–40 (especially 128–9).

12–13 *Si . . . mecum* 'If you know wiser precepts than these, be kind and tell me; if not, practise mine with me.' Horace, *Epistles*, I, vi.67–68

15 NICHOLAS OKES a printer whose shop – between 1610 and 1617 – was near Holborn Bridge, close to the premises of the Webster family's coaching business. He also printed Webster's *The White Devil*, *A Monumental Column* and *Monuments of Honour*.

THE
TRAGEDY

OF THE DVTCHESSE
Of Malfy.

As it was Presented priuatly, at the Black-
Friers; and publiquely at the Globe, By the
Kings Maiesties Seruants.

The perfect and exact Coppy, with diuerse
things Printed, that the length of the Play would
not beare in the Presentment.

VVritten by *John Webster.*

Hora.——*Si quid——*
——*Candidus Imperti si non his vtere mecum.*

LONDON:

Printed by NICHOLAS OKES, for IOHN
WATERSON, and are to be sold at the
signe of the Crowne, in *Paules*
Church-yard, *1623.*

The Actors' Names No previously published English play contains a cast list. The provision of two names for three roles indicates that this one refers to two separate productions: see Introduction, pp. xxxii–xxxiii.

6 *Forobosco* A 'ghost' (= non-speaking) character, referred to in II.ii.31 as keeper of the key of the park gate. He need not appear on stage. Though the wording of its title-page suggests that Q1 was longer than the acted version, the part of Forobosco may have been excised from the printed text. It is also possible that Towley's name should have appeared opposite 'Malateste': cf.ll.13–14n.

13–14 bracket: Lucas II; opposite ll. 14–15 in Q1

16 *Three young children* Few modern productions have three child actors. A doll, initially used in II.ii, usually later does duty as the Duchess's youngest child. In the 1985 NT production the play's time-span was reduced by the use of a single doll throughout the action, whose crying emanated from an off-stage recording. For the 1989/90 RSC production there were two children and a doll in Stratford; one child and two dolls in London – a situation which made the Duchess's concern for her little girl (IV.ii.201–02) appear strange.

The Actors' Names

Bosola, *J. Lowin.*
Ferdinand, 1. *R. Burbidge.* 2. *J. Taylor.*
Cardinal, 1. *H. Cundaile.* 2. *R. Robinson.*
Antonio, 1. *W. Ostler.* 2. *R. Benfield.*
Delio, *J. Underwood.*   5
Forobosco, *N. Towley.*
Malateste.
The Marquis of Pescara, *J. Rice.*
Silvio, *T. Pollard.*
The several madmen, *N. Towley, J. Underwood, etc.*   10
The Duchess, *R. Sharpe.*
The Cardinal's Mistress, *J. Tomson.*
The Doctor, ⎫
Cariola,   ⎬ *R. Pallant.*
Court Officers.   15
Three young children.
Two Pilgrims.

1–2 GEORGE HARDING, thirteenth Baron Berkeley, only twenty-two when Webster dedicated Q1 to him, was known as a good friend to the theatre in general and the King's Men in particular.

10 *conduct* conductor

13 *clearest* most complete, absolute

14 *ancientest* ed. (ancien'st Q1)

14–15 The source of this phrase, also used in *The Devil's Law-Case*, I.i.33–34, is Overbury's character 'A Wife' (1614): '*Gentry* is but a *relique* of Time past' (Dent, p. 290).

27–28 *approved censure* tried judgement

To the Right Honourable GEORGE HARDING, BARON
BERKELEY, *of Berkeley Castle and Knight of the Order*
of the Bath to the illustrious Prince CHARLES.

My Noble Lord,
    That I may present my excuse why, (being a stranger to   5
your Lordship) I offer this poem to your patronage, I
plead this warrant; men, who never saw the sea, yet desire
to behold that regiment of waters, choose some eminent river
to guide them thither; and make that as it were, their
conduct, or postilion. By the like ingenious means has   10
your fame arrived at my knowledge, receiving it from some
of worth, who both in contemplation, and practice, owe to
your Honour their clearest service. I do not altogether look
up at your title: The ancientest nobility, being but a relic of
time past, and the truest honour indeed being for a man to   15
confer honour on himself, which your learning strives to
propagate, and shall make you arrive at the dignity of a
great example. I am confident this work is not unworthy your
Honour's perusal for by such poems as this, poets have kissed
the hands of great princes, and drawn their gentle eyes to   20
look down upon their sheets of paper, when the poets themselves were bound up in their winding sheets. The like
courtesy from your Lordship, shall make you live in your
grave, and laurel spring out of it; when the ignorant scorners
of the Muses (that like worms in libraries, seem to live only,   25
to destroy learning) shall wither, neglected and forgotten.
This work and myself I humbly present to your approved
censure. It being the utmost of my wishes, to have your
honourable self my weighty and perspicuous comment:
which grace so done me, shall ever be acknowledged   30
          By your Lordship's
            in all duty and
             observance,
               John Webster.

In the just worth, of that well deserver
MR. JOHN WEBSTER, and upon this
masterpiece of tragedy.

In this thou imitat'st one rich, and wise,
That sees his good deeds done before he dies;   5
As he by works, thou by this work of fame,
Hast well provided for thy living name;
To trust to others' honourings, is worth's crime,
Thy monument is rais'd in thy life time;
And 'tis most just; for every worthy man   10
Is his own marble; and his merit can
Cut him to any figure, and express
More art, than Death's cathedral palaces,
Where royal ashes keep their court: thy note
Be ever plainness, 'tis the richest coat: 15
Thy epitaph only the title be,
Write, *Duchess*, that will fetch a tear for thee,
For who e'er saw this *Duchess* live, and die,
That could get off under a bleeding eye?

In Tragædiam.   20
Ut lux ex tenebris ictu percussa tonantis;
Illa, (ruina malis) claris sit vita poetis.
                          Thomas Middletonus,
                              Poëta & Chron:
                              Londinensis.   25

20–22   To Tragedy.
    As light from darkness is struck at the blow of the thunderer,
    May it (ruin to the evil) be life to famous poets.
24–25 *Chron. Londinensis* Chronologer of London. Thomas Middleton, a dra-
    matic collaborator with Webster (see Introduction, pp. xvi–xvii) was
    appointed City Chronologer in 1620.

To his friend MR JOHN WEBSTER
Upon his DUCHESS
OF MALFI.

I never saw thy Duchess, till the day,
That she was lively body'd in thy play;   5
Howe'er she answer'd her low-rated love,
Her brothers' anger did so fatal prove,
Yet my opinion is, she might speak more;
But never (in her life) so well before.
                    WIL: ROWLEY.   10

To the reader of the author,
and his DUCHESS OF MALFI

Crown him a poet, whom nor Rome, nor Greece,
Transcend in all theirs, for a masterpiece:
In which, whiles words and matter change, and men   15
Act one another; he, from whose clear pen
They all took life, to memory hath lent
A lasting fame, to raise his monument.
                    JOHN FORD

5 *body'd* embodied
6 *answer'd* justified
10, 19 William Rowley and John Ford were both dramatic collaborators with
      Webster: see Introduction, pp. xvi–xvii.
16 *clear* pure

[DRAMATIS PERSONAE]

BOSOLA, *gentleman of the horse*
FERDINAND, *Duke of Calabria*
CARDINAL, *his brother*
ANTONIO BOLOGNA, *steward of the Duchess's household*
DELIO, *his friend; a courtier*
FOROBOSCO
MALATESTE, *a Count*
THE MARQUIS OF PESCARA
SILVIO, *a Lord*
CASTRUCHIO, *an old Lord*
RODERIGO ⎱
GRISOLAN ⎰ *Lords*
THE DUCHESS
CARIOLA, *her waiting-woman*
JULIA, *wife to Castruchio and mistress to the Cardinal*
THE DOCTOR
COURT OFFICERS
EIGHT MADMEN: *Astrologer, Lawyer, Priest, Doctor, English Tailor,*
 Gentleman Usher, Farmer, Broker
OLD LADY
THREE YOUNG CHILDREN
TWO PILGRIMS
ATTENDANTS, LADIES, EXECUTIONERS]

[DRAMATIS PERSONAE] Qq1–2's list of Actors' Names is given on p. 3 above. Q3
 gives the cast of the production first presented by the Duke's Company in
 1664, with Betterton as Bosola and Mrs Betterton as the Duchess; Q4 that
 of the version of the play presented on 22 July 1707 at the Queen's Theatre
 in the Haymarket, with Verbruggen as Ferdinand and Keene as the Cardinal.
CASTRUCHIO Lucas notes that the name is derived from Bandello's historic
 Petrucci, Cardinal of Siena, whom Painter, following Belleforest,
 calls Castruccio. Webster may have given the name to Julia's old husband
 because it sounds as if it meant 'castrated'. Florio's gloss of *Castrone* as 'a
 gelded man … Also a noddie, a meacocke, [effeminate person] a cuckold, a
 ninnie, a gull' clearly applies to this character (Lucas II, 132).
CARIOLA Florio glosses *Carriolo* or *Carriuola* as, among other things, a 'trundle-
 bed'. G.K. Hunter points out that Webster's choice of the name was appropriate 'in an age when personal servants slept in trundle-beds close to their
 employers' beds' ('Notes on Webster's Tragedies', *N&Q* n.s. 4 (1957), 55).
EIGHT MADMEN Their professions are listed in IV.ii.46–59.
BROKER dealer

THE DUCHESS OF MALFI

Act I, Scene i

[Enter ANTONIO *and* DELIO]

DELIO

  You are welcome to your country, dear Antonio,
  You have been long in France, and you return
  A very formal Frenchman, in your habit.
  How do you like the French court?

ANTONIO   I admire it;

  In seeking to reduce both State and people   5
  To a fix'd order, their judicious King
  Begins at home. Quits first his royal palace
  Of flatt'ring sycophants, of dissolute,
  And infamous persons, which he sweetly terms
  His Master's master-piece, the work of Heaven,   10
  Consid'ring duly, that a Prince's court
  Is like a common fountain, whence should flow
  Pure silver-drops in general. But if't chance
  Some curs'd example poison't near the head,
  Death and diseases through the whole land spread.   15
  And what is't makes this blessed government,
  But a most provident Council, who dare freely
  Inform him, the corruption of the times?
  Though some o'th' court hold it presumption
  To instruct Princes what they ought to do,   20
  It is a noble duty to inform them
  What they ought to foresee. Here comes Bosola

[Enter BOSOLA]

Act I, Scene i The action up to the end of II.iii is set in the Duchess's palace at
Amalfi.

  3 *habit* dress

  6 *their* Qq3–4 (there Qq1–2)

  7 *Quits* rids

 13 *in general* everywhere

 18 *Inform him, the* inform him [about] the

The only court-gall: yet I observe his railing
Is not for simple love of piety:
Indeed he rails at those things which he wants,   25
Would be as lecherous, covetous, or proud,
Bloody, or envious, as any man,
If he had means to be so. Here's the Cardinal.

[*Enter* CARDINAL]

BOSOLA   I do haunt you still.
CARDINAL   So.   30
BOSOLA   I have done you better service than to be slighted
    thus. Miserable age, where only the reward of doing well,
    is the doing of it!
CARDINAL   You enforce your merit too much.
BOSOLA   I fell into the galleys in your service, where, for   35
    two years together, I wore two towels instead of a shirt,
    with a knot on the shoulder, after the fashion of a Roman
    mantle. Slighted thus? I will thrive some way: blackbirds
    fatten best in hard weather: why not I, in these dog days?
CARDINAL   Would you could become honest, –   40
BOSOLA   With all your divinity, do but direct me the way
    to it. I have known many travel far for it, and yet return
    as arrant knaves, as they went forth; because they carried
    themselves always along with them. [*Exit* CARDINAL] Are
    you gone? Some fellows, they say, are possessed with the   45
    devil, but this great fellow were able to possess the greatest
    devil, and make him worse.
ANTONIO   He hath denied thee some suit?
BOSOLA   He and his brother are like plum trees, that grow
    crooked over standing pools, they are rich, and o'erladen   50
    with fruit, but none but crows, pies, and caterpillars feed
    on them. Could I be one of their flatt'ring panders, I would
    hang on their ears like a horse-leech, till I were full, and
    then drop off. I pray leave me. Who would rely upon these
    miserable dependences, in expectation to be advanc'd   55
    tomorrow? What creature ever fed worse, than hoping

23 *court-gall* court sore-spot; gall = bitterness is also implicit
32 *only the reward* the only reward
34 *enforce* urge, emphasize
39 *dog days* evil or unhealthy times of hot weather, when Sirius, the dog-star,
   is high in the sky; usually 11 August–19 September
50 *standing* stagnant
51 *pies* magpies
53 *and* Qq2–4 (an Q1)
55 *dependences* appointments in reversion

Tantalus; nor ever died any man more fearfully, than he
that hop'd for a pardon? There are rewards for hawks, and
dogs, when they have done us service; but for a soldier, that
hazards his limbs in a battle, nothing but a kind of geo-   60
metry is his last supportation.

DELIO   Geometry?

BOSOLA   Ay, to hang in a fair pair of slings, take his latter
swing in the world, upon an honourable pair of crutches,
from hospital to hospital: fare ye well sir. And yet do not   65
you scorn us, for places in the court are but like beds in the
hospital, where this man's head lies at that man's foot, and
so lower and lower.   [*Exit* BOSOLA]

DELIO

I knew this fellow seven years in the galleys,
For a notorious murther, and 'twas thought   70
The Cardinal suborn'd it: he was releas'd
By the French general, Gaston de Foix
When he recover'd Naples.

ANTONIO   'Tis great pity
He should be thus neglected, I have heard
He's very valiant. This foul melancholy   75
Will poison all his goodness, for, I'll tell you,
If too immoderate sleep be truly said
To be an inward rust unto the soul;
It then doth follow want of action
Breeds all black malcontents, and their close rearing,   80
Like moths in cloth, do hurt for want of wearing.

57 *Tantalus* had to stand up to his neck in water, unable to grasp the fruit above
his head: hence the name for a locked decanter and the origin of the verb
'to tantalize'.
died Q1b (did Q1a)
58 *pardon* Q1b (pleadon Q1a)
59 *and dogs,* Qq2–4 (dogs, and Q1)
60–61 *a kind of geometry* hanging awkwardly and stiffly from crutches, which
are thus likened to a pair of compasses or dividers
66 *like* Qq2–4 (likes Q1)
70 *murther* Qq1–2 (murtherer Qq3–4)
72 *Gaston de Foix* was aged 12 when Naples was recovered in 1501.
Foix Q4 (Foux Q1; Foyx Q2; Fox Q3)

Scene ii Qq have no *Exeunt* after I.i.81 and some editors (from Dyce to Brown)
leave Act I undivided, though 'SCENA II' is clearly marked and Antonio and Delio
are included in its block entry. As an *Exit* appears to have dropped from the text
at II.iii.76, an *Exeunt* may have been lost here. Though they need not leave the
stage, the reappearance of Antonio and Delio with other courtiers gives an
impression of the size of the Duchess's palace and indicates the friends' progress
towards her presence chamber.

Scene ii

[*Enter* CASTRUCHIO, SILVIO, RODERIGO *and* GRISOLAN]

DELIO
  The presence 'gins to fill. You promis'd me
  To make me the partaker of the natures
  Of some of your great courtiers.
ANTONIO   The Lord Cardinal's
  And other strangers', that are now in court?
  I shall. Here comes the great Calabrian Duke.   5

[*Enter* FERDINAND]

FERDINAND   Who took the ring oft'nest?
SILVIO   Antonio Bologna, my lord.
FERDINAND   Our sister Duchess' great master of her house-
  hold? Give him the jewel: when shall we leave this sportive
  action, and fall to action indeed?   10
CASTRUCHIO   Methinks, my lord, you should not desire to
  go to war, in person.
FERDINAND [*Aside*] Now, for some gravity: why, my lord?
CASTRUCHIO   It is fitting a soldier arise to be a prince, but
  not necessary a prince descend to be a captain!   15
FERDINAND   No?
CASTRUCHIO   No, my lord, he were far better do it by a
  deputy.
FERDINAND   Why should he not as well sleep, or eat, by a
  deputy? This might take idle, offensive, and base office from   20
  him, whereas the other deprives him of honour.
CASTRUCHIO   Believe my experience: that realm is never
  long in quiet, where the ruler is a soldier.
FERDINAND   Thou told'st me thy wife could not endure
  fighting.   25
CASTRUCHIO   True, my lord.

---

1 *presence* presence or audience chamber
6 *took the ring* i.e. in jousting; a bawdy pun may also be implicit. Cf. Dekker
  and Webster, *Northward Ho!* I.iii.91–92: 'Know'st thou this ring? there has
  been old running at the ring since I went' (Bowers II, p. 422). There are
  obvious associations with other examples of the ring as both image and
  object in the play. The 1972 BBC television production opened with the
  swift taking of a hempen ring which was suspended like a noose, thus making
  the audience painfully aware of the play's juxtaposition of love and death.
11 *should not* Q1, Q4 (should Qq2–3)
17 *do it* Q1, Q4 (to do it Qq2–3)

FERDINAND   And of a jest she broke, of a captain she met
    full of wounds: I have forgot it.
CASTRUCHIO   She told him, my lord, he was a pitiful fellow,
    to lie, like the children of Israel, all in tents.   30
FERDINAND   Why, there's a wit were able to undo all the
    chirurgeons o' the city, for although gallants should quarrel,
    and had drawn their weapons, and were ready to go to it;
    yet her persuasions would make them put up.
CASTRUCHIO   That she would, my lord.   35
FERDINAND   How do you like my Spanish jennet?
RODERIGO   He is all fire.
FERDINAND   I am of Pliny's opinion, I think he was begot
    by the wind; he runs as if he were ballass'd with quick-
    silver.   40
SILVIO   True, my lord, he reels from the tilt often.
RODERIGO *and* GRISOLAN   Ha, ha, ha!
FERDINAND   Why do you laugh? Methinks you that are
    courtiers should be my touchwood, take fire when I give
    fire; that is, laugh when I laugh, were the subject never so   45
    witty, –
CASTRUCHIO   True, my lord, I myself have heard a very
    good jest, and have scorn'd to seem to have so silly a wit, as
    to understand it.

27 *jest she broke, of* joke she cracked, about
30 *Israel* this edn (Ismael Qq): see Additional Notes, p. 133.
    tents usual meaning; dressings for wounds
32 *chirurgeons* surgeons
34 *put up* sheathe their weapons. Ferdinand continues this vein of innuendo in
    conversation with his sister: see I.ii.249–57n.
36 s.p. conj. Sampson; Brown added that the line is inset 'as if Compositor B
    had placed a space in his composing-stick intending to set a speech-prefix
    and then forgotten to add it' (p. 16). Moreover, by both rank and inclination,
    Ferdinand is the initiator of dialogue.
36 *jennet* a light Spanish horse
38 *Pliny's opinion* was that in Portugal, along the River Tagus and about Lisbon,
    mares conceived from the west wind and brought forth foals as swift as the
    wind. See Holland's translation of Pliny's *Natural History* (1601) VIII,
    chapter 42, p. 222.
39 *ballass'd* ballasted
41 *reels from the tilt* jibs and refuses to (1) run at the ring in jousting; (2) copulate
44 *touchwood* tinder
45 *laugh when I laugh* Qq1–3 (Not laugh but when I laugh Q4) In 'Webster:
    Another Borrowing from Jonson's *Sejanus*?', *N&Q* n.s. 17 (1970), 214,
    D.C. Gunby sees a parallel in Sicilius's description of Sejanus's clients as
    able to 'Laugh, when their patron laughs; sweat, when he sweates;/ Be hot,
    and cold, with him;' *Sejanus* I, 33–34.
48 *silly* simple

FERDINAND   But I can laugh at your fool, my lord.   50
CASTRUCHIO   He cannot speak, you know, but he makes
  faces; my lady cannot abide him.
FERDINAND   No?
CASTRUCHIO   Nor endure to be in merry company: for she
  says too much laughing, and too much company, fills her   55
  too full of the wrinkle.
FERDINAND   I would then have a mathematical instrument
  made for her face, that she might not laugh out of compass.
  I shall shortly visit you at Milan, Lord Silvio.
SILVIO   Your Grace shall arrive most welcome.   60
FERDINAND   You are a good horseman, Antonio; you have
  excellent riders in France, what do you think of good
  horsemanship?
ANTONIO   Nobly, my lord: as out of the Grecian horse
  issued many famous princes: so out of brave horsemanship,   65
  arise the first sparks of growing resolution, that raise the
  mind to noble action.
FERDINAND   You have bespoke it worthily.

[*Enter* DUCHESS, CARDINAL, CARIOLA *and* JULIA]

SILVIO   Your brother, the Lord Cardinal, and sister
  Duchess.   70
CARDINAL   Are the galleys come about?
GRISOLAN   They are, my lord.
FERDINAND   Here's the Lord Silvio, is come to take his
  leave.
DELIO [*Aside to* ANTONIO] Now sir, your promise: what's   75
  that Cardinal? I mean his temper? They say he's a brave
  fellow, will play his five thousand crowns at tennis, dance,
  court ladies, and one that hath fought single combats.

54–56 Just as ll. 31–34 reveal Ferdinand's opinion of Julia's nature as well as
  her wit, so these lines reveal both her jesting attitude to adultery and the
  way Castruchio is duped by it. Cf. II.iv.3–5.
56 *wrinkle* crease; moral blemish
57–58 Cf. Dekker and Webster, *Westward Ho!* I.i.77–78: 'no German Clock
  nor Mathematicall Ingin whatsoeuer requires so much reparation as a
  womans face...' (Bowers II, p. 321).
58 *out of compass* beyond the bounds of moderation
68 s.d. Lucas comments that the only real uncertainty raised by the block entry
  for SCENA II concerns the point where Julia enters: here, with her lover the
  Cardinal, or earlier, with her husband. Her entry here underlines both her
  contrast with the Duchess and the basis for Ferdinand's earlier innuendo.
71 *come about* come round in the opposite direction, i.e. returned to port

ANTONIO   Some such flashes superficially hang on him, for
   form: but observe his inward character: he is a melancholy   80
   churchman. The spring in his face is nothing but the engen-
   d'ring of toads: where he is jealous of any man, he lays
   worse plots for them, than ever was impos'd on Hercules:
   for he strews in his way flatterers, panders, intelligencers,
   atheists: and a thousand such political monsters: he   85
   should have been Pope: but instead of coming to it by the
   primitive decency of the Church, he did bestow bribes, so
   largely, and so impudently, as if he would have carried it
   away without Heaven's knowledge. Some good he hath done.
DELIO
   You have given too much of him: what's his brother?   90
ANTONIO
   The Duke there? a most perverse and turbulent nature;
   What appears in him mirth, is merely outside,
   If he laugh heartily, it is to laugh
   All honesty out of fashion.
DELIO   Twins?
ANTONIO   In quality:
   He speaks with others' tongues, and hears men's suits   95
   With others' ears: will seem to sleep o'th' bench
   Only to entrap offenders in their answers;
   Dooms men to death by information,
   Rewards, by hearsay.
DELIO   Then the law to him
   Is like a foul black cobweb to a spider,   100
   He makes it his dwelling, and a prison
   To entangle those shall feed him.
ANTONIO   Most true:
   He nev'r pays debts, unless they be shrewd turns,
   And those he will confess, that he doth owe.
   Last: for his brother, there, the Cardinal,   105
   They that do flatter him most, say oracles
   Hang at his lips: and verily I believe them:
   For the devil speaks in them.

---

79 *flashes* examples of ostentatious display
81 *spring* i.e. of water
84 *flatterers* Qq3–4 (flatters Qq1–2)
   intelligencers informers, spies
85 *political* scheming
94 *Twins?* Q1 (Twins. Qq2–4) In the 1971 and 1989/90 RSC productions the
   physical resemblance between the Duchess and her brothers was suggested
   by casting, costuming and/or hair colouring.
103 *shrewd* Qq2–3 (shewed Q1; Q4 *omits*); *shrewd turns* malicious deeds

But for their sister, the right noble Duchess,
You never fix'd your eye on three fair medals,   110
Cast in one figure, of so different temper.
For her discourse, it is so full of rapture,
You only will begin, then to be sorry
When she doth end her speech: and wish, in wonder,
She held it less vainglory to talk much   115
Than you penance, to hear her: whilst she speaks,
She throws upon a man so sweet a look,
That it were able to raise one to a galliard
That lay in a dead palsy; and to dote
On that sweet countenance: but in that look   120
There speaketh so divine a continence,
As cuts off all lascivious, and vain hope.
Her days are practis'd in such noble virtue,
That, sure her nights, nay more, her very sleeps,
Are more in heaven, than other ladies' shrifts.   125
Let all sweet ladies break their flatt'ring glasses,
And dress themselves in her.
DELIO   Fie Antonio,
You play the wire-drawer with her commendations.
ANTONIO
I'll case the picture up: only thus much:
All her particular worth grows to this sum: 130
She stains the time past: lights the time to come.
CARIOLA
You must attend my lady, in the gallery,
Some half an hour hence.
ANTONIO   I shall.

                              [*Exeunt* ANTONIO *and* DELIO]

110 *your* Qq2–4 (you Q1)
111 *figure* form, shape
      temper combination of elements
112–27 On Webster's source for these lines see Additional Notes, pp. 133–34.
116 *you* Anderson (your Qq1–3; Q4 *omits*) As Brown indicates (p. 20), Marcia
      Lee Anderson's identification of Webster's source resolved this textual crux.
118 *able to* Qq3–4 (able Qq1–2)
      galliard a lively dance
125 *shrifts* confessions
128 *play the wire-drawer* spin out, over-refine
131 From Sir William Alexander's *Alexandrean Tragedy* III.ii. 1319: 'Staine of
      times past, and light of times to come' (Dent, p. 185)
      stains throws into the shade, eclipses

FERDINAND

Sister, I have a suit to you.

DUCHESS   To me, sir?

FERDINAND

A gentleman here: Daniel de Bosola: 135
One, that was in the galleys.

DUCHESS   Yes, I know him.

FERDINAND

A worthy fellow h'is: pray let me entreat for
The provisorship of your horse.

DUCHESS   Your knowledge of him
Commends him, and prefers him.

FERDINAND   Call him hither.

                              [*Exit* ATTENDANT]

We are now upon parting. Good Lord Silvio   140
Do us commend to all our noble friends
At the leaguer.

SILVIO   Sir, I shall.

DUCHESS

You are for Milan?

SILVIO   I am.

DUCHESS

Bring the caroches: we'll bring you down to the haven.

          [*Exeunt* DUCHESS, CARIOLA, SILVIO, CASTRUCHIO, RODERIGO,

                                   GRISOLAN *and* JULIA]

CARDINAL

Be sure you entertain that Bosola   145
For your intelligence: I would not be seen in't.
And therefore many times I have slighted him,
When he did court our furtherance: as this morning.

FERDINAND

Antonio, the great master of her household
Had been far fitter.

CARDINAL   You are deceiv'd in him,   150

---

137 *entreat for* Qq (entreat for him   Lucas conj.)
140 *are now* Q4, Hazlitt (now Qq1–3; [are] now   Dyce, Vaughan, Sampson,
     Lucas; now are   McIlwraith, Brown)
142 *leaguer* Qq2–3 (leagues Q1; camp Q4) military camp
143 s.p. DUCHESS ed. (*Ferd.* Qq, Dyce, Hazlitt, Vaughan) Sampson pointed out
     that Ferdinand already knows that Silvio is going to Milan. If the Duchess
     asks the question, Silvio's reply allows her to offer to conduct him to the
     haven.
144 *caroches* large coaches
146 *For your intelligence* for supplying you with secret information
147 *I have* Qq1–2 (have I Q3; have Q4)

His nature is too honest for such business.
He comes: I'll leave you.

[*Enter* BOSOLA]

BOSOLA   I was lur'd to you. [*Exit* CARDINAL]
FERDINAND
My brother here, the Cardinal, could never
Abide you.
BOSOLA   Never since he was in my debt.
FERDINAND
May be some oblique character in your face   155
Made him suspect you?
BOSOLA   Doth he study physiognomy?
There's no more credit to be given to th' face,
Than to a sick man's urine, which some call
The physician's whore, because she cozens him.
He did suspect me wrongfully.
FERDINAND   For that   160
You must give great men leave to take their times:
Distrust doth cause us seldom be deceiv'd;
You see, the oft shaking of the cedar tree
Fastens it more at root.
BOSOLA   Yet take heed:
For to suspect a friend unworthily   165
Instructs him the next way to suspect you,
And prompts him to deceive you.
FERDINAND   There's gold.
BOSOLA   So:
What follows? (Never rain'd such showers as these
Without thunderbolts i'th' tail of them;)
Whose throat must I cut?   170
FERDINAND
Your inclination to shed blood rides post
Before my occasion to use you. I give you that
To live i'th' court, here: and observe the Duchess,
To note all the particulars of her 'haviour:
What suitors do solicit her for marriage   175
And whom she best affects: she's a young widow,
I would not have her marry again.

166 *next* nearest
168–69 Bosola here refers to the story of the transformation of Jupiter the
    Thunderer into a shower of gold to enable him to reach Danae in her brazen
    tower. Cf. II.ii. 18–20n.
171 *post* in haste
174 *'haviour* ed. (haviour Qq1–2; behaviour Qq3–4) estate; behaviour

BOSOLA   No, sir?
FERDINAND
  Do not you ask the reason: but be satisfied,
  I say I would not.
BOSOLA   It seems you would create me
  One of your familiars.
FERDINAND   Familiar? what's that?   180
BOSOLA
  Why, a very quaint invisible devil in flesh:
  An intelligencer.
FERDINAND   Such a kind of thriving thing
  I would wish thee: and ere long, thou mayst arrive
  At a higher place by't.
BOSOLA   Take your devils
  Which hell calls angels: these curs'd gifts would make   185
  You a corrupter, me an impudent traitor,
  And should I take these they'll'd take me to hell.
FERDINAND
  Sir, I'll take nothing from you that I have given.
  There is a place that I procur'd for you
  This morning, the provisorship o'th' horse,   190
  Have you heard on't?
BOSOLA   No.
FERDINAND   'Tis yours, is't not worth thanks?
BOSOLA
  I would have you curse yourself now, that your bounty,
  Which makes men truly noble, e'er should make
  Me a villain: oh, that to avoid ingratitude
  For the good deed you have done me, I must do   195
  All the ill man can invent. Thus the devil
  Candies all sins o'er: and what Heaven terms vild,
  That names he complemental.
FERDINAND   Be yourself:
  Keep your old garb of melancholy: 'twill express
  You envy those that stand above your reach,   200
  Yet strive not to come near 'em. This will gain
  Access to private lodgings, where yourself

184–87 One is here reminded of Judas Iscariot.
185 *angels* gold coins bearing the image of St Michael killing the dragon
187 *to hell* Q4 (hell Qq1–3)
191 *on't* Qq3–4 (out Q1; ont Q2). Cf. III.ii.100.
197 *Candies . . . o'er* sugars . . . over; *o'er* ed. (are Q1; ore Qq2–4)
     vild Qq1–2 (vile Qq3–4)
198 *complemental* accomplished
203 *politic* crafty, scheming

May, like a politic dormouse, –
BOSOLA   As I have seen some,
Feed in a lord's dish, half asleep, not seeming
To listen to any talk: and yet these rogues   205
Have cut his throat in a dream: what's my place?
The provisorship o'th' horse? say then my corruption
Grew out of horse dung. I am your creature.
FERDINAND
Away!
BOSOLA
Let good men, for good deeds, covet good fame,   210
Since place and riches oft are bribes of shame;
Sometimes the devil doth preach.   *Exit* BOSOLA.

[*Enter* CARDINAL, DUCHESS *and* CARIOLA]

CARDINAL
We are to part from you: and your own discretion
Must now be your director.
FERDINAND   You are a widow:
You know already what man is: and therefore   215
Let not youth, high promotion, eloquence, –

insatiable appetite cant go back [handwritten annotation]

CARDINAL
No, nor any thing without the addition, Honour,
Sway your high blood.
FERDINAND   Marry? they are most luxurious,
Will wed twice.
CARDINAL   O fie!
FERDINAND   Their livers are more spotted
Than Laban's sheep.
DUCHESS   Diamonds are of most value   220
They say, that have pass'd through most jewellers' hands.

---

204 *Feed ... dish* dine at a lord's table (Brown)
207 *provisorship* Q1b (Prouisors-ship) (Prouisosr-ship Q1a) office of responsibility for provisioning, etc.
210–12 P. Haworth, *English Hymns and Ballads* relates this passage to Antonio's description of the French court, and concludes, 'Bosola's speech seems therefore to express the moral purpose Webster had in view in treating the story' (pp. 116–17).
213 Sampson marks Scene ii here.
218 *high blood* noble breeding; passionate nature: cf. *The White Devil* V.vi. 237–38
    luxurious lascivious
219 *livers* The liver was thought to be the seat of violent passions, like love. Cf. *As You Like It* III.ii. 441–44.
220 *Laban's sheep* See Genesis 30.31–42 and cf. *The Merchant of Venice* I.iii. 66–85.   221 *pass'd* ed. (past Qq)

FERDINAND
  Whores, by that rule, are precious.
DUCHESS   Will you hear me?
  I'll never marry –
CARDINAL   So most widows say:
  But commonly that motion lasts no longer
  Than the turning of an hourglass; the funeral sermon   225
  And it, end both together.
FERDINAND   Now hear me:
  You live in a rank pasture here, i'th' court,
  There is a kind of honey-dew that's deadly:
  'Twill poison your fame; look to't; be not cunning:
  For they whose faces do belie their hearts   230
  Are witches, ere they arrive at twenty years,
  Ay: and give the devil suck.
DUCHESS   This is terrible good counsel.
FERDINAND
  Hypocrisy is woven of a fine small thread,
  Subtler than Vulcan's engine: yet, believe't,
  Your darkest actions: nay, your privat'st thoughts,   235
  Will come to light.
CARDINAL   You may flatter yourself,
  And take your own choice: privately be married
  Under the eaves of night –
FERDINAND   Think't the best voyage
  That e'er you made; like the irregular crab,
  Which, though't goes backward, thinks that it goes right,   240
  Because it goes its own way: but observe:
  Such weddings may more properly be said
  To be executed, than celebrated.
CARDINAL   The marriage night

224 *motion* resolution
227–28 Q1 punctuation allows for two interpretations: (1) You live in a rank
     pasture here, i'th court:/ There is . . .; (2) You live in a rank pasture: here,
     i'th court/ There is. . .
228 *honey-dew* sweet, sticky substance, excreted by aphides on leaves and stems,
     formerly believed to be a kind of dew. W. L. Godshalk, 'Shakespeare's
     Honey-Stalks: Webster's Honey-Dew', *N&Q* n.s. 26 (1979), 114–15, sug-
     gests that Webster found 'honey-stalks', referred to in *Titus Andronicus* IV.iv.
     89–93, incomprehensible. By substitution, he formed an image of dew
     'covering *stalks* of vegetation' (p. 115).
234 *Vulcan's engine* the net – so fine it was virtually invisible – wherein he caught
     his wife, Venus, with Mars
238 *eaves* ed. (Eeues Q1a; Eues Q1b; Eves Qq2–4)
243 *executed; celebrated* Both denote the performance of religious rites. The
     connotation of punishment by death as opposed to rejoicing is implicit in
     Ferdinand's distinction between them.

Is the entrance into some prison.

FERDINAND   And those joys,

  Those lustful pleasures, are like heavy sleeps   245

  Which do forerun man's mischief.

CARDINAL   Fare you well.

  Wisdom begins at the end: remember it.   [*Exit* CARDINAL]

DUCHESS

  I think this speech between you both was studied,

  It came so roundly off.

FERDINAND   You are my sister,

  This was my father's poniard: do you see,   250

  I'll'd be loath to see't look rusty, 'cause 'twas his.

  I would have you to give o'er these chargeable revels;

  A visor and a mask are whispering-rooms

  That were nev'r built for goodness: fare ye well:

  And women like that part, which, like the lamprey,   255

  Hath nev'r a bone in't.

DUCHESS   Fie sir!

FERDINAND   Nay,

  I mean the tongue: variety of courtship;

  What cannot a neat knave with a smooth tale

  Make a woman believe? Farewell, lusty widow.

                                        [*Exit* FERDINAND]

DUCHESS

  Shall this move me? If all my royal kindred   260

  Lay in my way unto this marriage:

  I'll'd make them my low foot-steps. And even now,

  Even in this hate, (as men in some great battles

  By apprehending danger, have achiev'd

249–57 For the sexual implications of Ferdinand's action and words see *Northward Ho!* I.ii. 6–7 and V.i. 356–57 (Bowers II, pp. 417, 473) and cf. III. ii. 68–75 below, where 'tongue', the poniard and 'bare' all occur.

251 *I'll'd* Q1 (I'd Qq2–4)
   see't Q1 (see it Qq2–4)

252 *to* Q1 (Qq2–4 *omit*)
   chargeable expensive

255 *women* Q2 (woemen Q1; woman Q3; Q4 *omits*)
   lamprey an eel-like fish

258 *neat* finely dressed; free from disease

260ff. In 'Sexual and Social Mobility in *The Duchess of Malfi*', *PMLA* 100 (1985), 167–86 Frank Whigham points out that the Duchess's language here, with its use of heroic topoi, has tones that are 'martial, not erotic' (p. 171).

262 *I'll'd* Q1 (I'd Qq2–4)·
   foot-steps stepping stones

Almost impossible actions: I have heard soldiers say so,)   265
So I, through frights and threat'nings, will assay
This dangerous venture. Let old wives report
I winked, and chose a husband. Cariola,
To thy known secrecy I have given up
More than my life, my fame.
CARIOLA   Both shall be safe: 270
For I'll conceal this secret from the world
As warily as those that trade in poison,
Keep poison from their children.
DUCHESS   Thy protestation
Is ingenious and hearty: I believe it.
Is Antonio come?
CARIOLA   He attends you.
DUCHESS   Good dear soul,   275
Leave me: but place thyself behind the arras,
Where thou mayst overhear us: wish me good speed
For I am going into a wilderness,
Where I shall find nor path, nor friendly clew
To be my guide.

> [CARIOLA *goes behind the arras; the* DUCHESS *draws the*
> *traverse to reveal* ANTONIO]

          I sent for you. Sit down: 280
Take pen and ink, and write. Are you ready?
ANTONIO   Yes.
DUCHESS
What did I say?
ANTONIO   That I should write somewhat.
DUCHESS
Oh, I remember:
After these triumphs and this large expense

---

266 *assay* Q1, Q4 (affray Qq2–3)
268 *winked* closed my eyes; closed my eyes to something wrong. Brown places
     Cariola's entrance here, thereby making ll. 260–68 a soliloquy. If Cariola
     has entered earlier, the lines indicate the Duchess's trust in and dependence
     on Cariola, both of which will grow in the coming action.
274 *ingenious* usual meaning; ingenuous
279 *nor* Q1 (no Qq2–4)   *clew* thread to guide one through a labyrinth
280 s.d. *traverse* curtain on runners
280ff. Clifford Leech noted 'we are now "in the gallery" where Antonio was
     earlier told to see her: the locality has changed without a break in the action'
     (*Webster: 'The Duchess of Malfi'*, p. 12).
284 *these triumphs* Dyce (this triumphs Qq1–2; this triumph Qq3–4)
     triumphs festivities, i.e. the chargeable revels of l. 252 above

It's fit, like thrifty husbands, we inquire   285
What's laid up for tomorrow.

ANTONIO
So please your beauteous excellence.

DUCHESS   Beauteous?
Indeed I thank you: I look young for your sake.
You have tane my cares upon you.

ANTONIO   I'll fetch your Grace
The particulars of your revenue and expense.   290

DUCHESS
Oh, you are an upright treasurer: but you mistook,
For when I said I meant to make inquiry
What's laid up for tomorrow: I did mean
What's laid up yonder for me.

ANTONIO   Where?

DUCHESS   In heaven.
I am making my will, as 'tis fit princes should   295
In perfect memory, and I pray sir, tell me
Were not one better make it smiling, thus?
Than in deep groans, and terrible ghastly looks,
As if the gifts we parted with, procur'd
That violent distraction?

ANTONIO   Oh, much better.   300

DUCHESS
If I had a husband now, this care were quit:
But I intend to make you overseer;
What good deed shall we first remember? Say.

ANTONIO
Begin with that first good deed, began i'th' world,
After man's creation, the sacrament of marriage.   305
I'ld have you first provide for a good husband,
Give him all.

DUCHESS   All?

ANTONIO   Yes, your excellent self.

DUCHESS
In a winding sheet?

ANTONIO   In a couple.

285 *husbands* usual meaning; stewards
290 *revenue* Qq3–4 (reuinew Q1; revenew Q2)
300 *distraction* Qq3–4 (distruction Qq1–2)
302 *you* Qq2–4 (yon Q1)
304 *that first good deed* Q1 (that good deed that first Qq2–4)
306 *first provide* Q1 (provide Qq2–4)
307 *him* Qq1–2 (me Q3; Q4 *omits*)
308 *couple* a pàir; marriage

DUCHESS

St. Winifred! that were a strange will.

ANTONIO   'Twere strange

If there were no will in you to marry again.   310

DUCHESS

What do you think of marriage?

ANTONIO

I take't, as those that deny purgatory,

It locally contains or heaven, or hell;

There's no third place in't.

DUCHESS   How do you affect it?

ANTONIO

My banishment, feeding my melancholy,   315

Would often reason thus: –

DUCHESS   Pray let's hear it.

ANTONIO

Say a man never marry, nor have children,

What takes that from him? only the bare name

Of being a father, or the weak delight

To see the little wanton ride a-cock-horse   320

Upon a painted stick, or hear him chatter

Like a taught starling.

DUCHESS   Fie, fie, what's all this?

One of your eyes is bloodshot, use my ring to't,

They say 'tis very sovereign: 'twas my wedding ring,

And I did vow never to part with it,   325

But to my second husband.

ANTONIO

You have parted with it now.

DUCHESS   Yes, to help your eyesight.

ANTONIO

You have made me stark blind.

DUCHESS   How?

---

309 *St. Winifred* Dyce (St. Winfrid Qq, Sampson). Winifred (Gwenfrewi) was a
seventh-century Welsh saint whose head was struck off by Caradoc ap Alauc
for rejecting his advances. St Beuno, who was her mother's brother, restored
her to life, but from the place where her head fell there issued a spring
which gives its name to Holywell, Flintshire. St Winifred would have been
known to English audiences. St Winfred – or Wynfrith – was universally
known as St Boniface.

312 *those who deny purgatory* i.e. Protestants

314 *affect* like

320 *wanton* rogue (a term of endearment)

324 *sovereign* efficacious

ANTONIO
  There is a saucy and ambitious devil
  Is dancing in this circle.
DUCHESS   Remove him.
ANTONIO   How?   330
DUCHESS
  There needs small conjuration, when your finger
  May do it: thus, is it fit?
                    [*She puts the ring on his finger*] *he kneels.*
ANTONIO   What said you?
DUCHESS   Sir,
  This goodly roof of yours, is too low built,
  I cannot stand upright in't, nor discourse,
  Without I raise it higher: raise yourself,   335
  Or if you please, my hand to help you: so.   [*Raises him*]
ANTONIO
  Ambition, Madam, is a great man's madness,
  That is not kept in chains, and close-pent rooms,
  But in fair lightsome lodgings, and is girt
  With the wild noise of prattling visitants,   340
  Which makes it lunatic, beyond all cure.
  Conceive not, I am so stupid, but I aim
  Whereto your favours tend. But he's a fool
  That, being a-cold, would thrust his hands i'th' fire
  To warm them.
DUCHESS   So, now the ground's broke,   345
  You may discover what a wealthy mine
  I make you lord of.
ANTONIO   O my unworthiness!
DUCHESS
  You were ill to sell yourself;
  This dark'ning of your worth is not like that
  Which tradesmen use i'th' city; their false lights   350
  Are to rid bad wares off: and I must tell you
  If you will know where breathes a complete man,
  (I speak it without flattery), turn your eyes,
  And progress through yourself.

337–41 Just as the Duchess's references to her will, a winding sheet and her
      husband's tomb foreshadow death, so these of Antonio adumbrate the
      horrors which precede it.
340 *visitants* Qq3–4 (visitans Qq1–2)
342 *aim* guess, conjecture
347 *of* Qq2–4 (off Q1)
349 *dark'ning* obscuring
352 *will* Q1 (would Qq2–4)

ANTONIO   Were there nor heaven, nor hell,
  I should be honest: I have long serv'd virtue,   355
  And nev'r tane wages of her.
DUCHESS   Now she pays it.
  The misery of us, that are born great,
  We are forc'd to woo, because none dare woo us:
  And as a tyrant doubles with his words,
  And fearfully equivocates: so we   360
  Are forc'd to express our violent passions
  In riddles, and in dreams, and leave the path
  Of simple virtue, which was never made
  To seem the thing it is not. Go, go brag
  You have left me heartless, mine is in your bosom,   365
  I hope 'twill multiply love there. You do tremble:
  Make not your heart so dead a piece of flesh
  To fear, more than to love me. Sir, be confident,
  What is't distracts you? This is flesh, and blood, sir,
  'Tis not the figure cut in alabaster   370
  Kneels at my husband's tomb. Awake, awake, man,
  I do here put off all vain ceremony,
  And only do appear to you, a young widow
  That claims you for her husband, and like a widow,
  I use but half a blush in't.
ANTONIO   Truth speak for me,   375
  I will remain the constant sanctuary
  Of your good name.
DUCHESS   I thank you, gentle love,
  And 'cause you shall not come to me in debt,
  Being now my steward, here upon your lips
  I sign your *Quietus est*. This you should have begg'd now: 380
  I have seen children oft eat sweetmeats thus,
  As fearful to devour them too soon.
ANTONIO
  But for your brothers?
DUCHESS   Do not think of them:
  All discord, without this circumference,

---

358 *woo...woo* Q3 (woe...woe Qq1–2; wooe...wooe Q4). Both senses are
    implicit in the equivocal spellings here.
359 *doubles* acts evasively or deceitfully
372 *off* Qq2–4 (of Q1)
380 *Quietus est* In an account book, the phrase indicated that the accounts were
    correctly discharged; it was also used of the release of death, as in *Hamlet*
    III.i. 75.
381–82 Repeated in *Appius and Virginia* I.i. 20–21: see Dent, p. 191.
384 *this circumference* See Introduction, pp. xxii–xxiii, and cf. V.ii. 162.

Is only to be pitied, and not fear'd.   385
Yet, should they know it, time will easily
Scatter the tempest.

ANTONIO   These words should be mine,
And all the parts you have spoke, if some part of it
Would not have savour'd flattery.

DUCHESS   Kneel.

[*Enter* CARIOLA]

ANTONIO   Ha?

DUCHESS

Be not amaz'd, this woman's of my counsel.   390
I have heard lawyers say, a contract in a chamber,
Per verba de presenti, is absolute marriage.
Bless, Heaven, this sacred Gordian, which let violence
Never untwine.

ANTONIO

And may our sweet affections, like the spheres,   395
Be still in motion.

DUCHESS   Quick'ning, and make
The like soft music.

ANTONIO

That we may imitate the loving palms,
Best emblem of a peaceful marriage,
That nev'r bore fruit divided.   400

389 *savour'd* Q1 (favour'd Qq2–3; savour'd of Q4)
392 *Per verba de presenti* Sampson (Per verba presenti Qq): 'by words about the
     present'. A couple declaring their intention of marrying at the present
     moment were legally married. The church recognized the union as binding,
     though sinful. See Additional Note on "The Duchess of Malfi's Marriage",
     pp. 134–35.
393 *Heaven* See III.v. 79–80n.
     Gordian The oracle decreed that the person who loosed the knot tied by
     King Gordius of Phrygia would rule Asia. Alexander the Great cut it with
     his sword. Webster probably recalled Marston's *The Insatiate Countess* II.i:
     see D.C. Gunby, 'Further Borrowings by Webster?', *N&Q* n.s. 13 (1966),
     296–97.
395 *spheres* The planetary spheres were thought by the older astronomers to
     revolve round the earth, carrying with them the heavenly bodies and pro-
     ducing harmonious music.
396 *still* always
     quick'ning coming alive. Cf. IV. ii. 249.
398–400 This idea, derived from Pliny's *Natural History*, came to symbolize a
     peaceful – and therefore perfect – marriage.
398, 402 Antonio's petitions recall those of the Anglican Litany.

DUCHESS

What can the Church force more?

ANTONIO

That Fortune may not know an accident
Either of joy or sorrow, to divide
Our fixed wishes.

DUCHESS   How can the Church bind faster?

We now are man and wife, and 'tis the Church   405
That must but echo this. Maid, stand apart,
I now am blind.

ANTONIO   What's your conceit in this?

DUCHESS

I would have you lead your fortune by the hand,
Unto your marriage bed:
(You speak in me this, for we now are one)   410
We'll only lie, and talk together, and plot
T'appease my humorous kindred; and if you please,
Like the old tale, in *Alexander and Lodowick*,
Lay a naked sword between us, keep us chaste.
Oh, let me shroud my blushes in your bosom,   415
Since 'tis the treasury of all my secrets.

CARIOLA

Whether the spirit of greatness, or of woman
Reign most in her, I know not, but it shows
A fearful madness: I owe her much of pity.   *Exeunt.*

Act II, Scene i

[*Enter* BOSOLA *and* CASTRUCHIO]

BOSOLA   You say you would fain be taken for an eminent
courtier?

CASTRUCHIO   'Tis the very main of my ambition.

---

401 *force* enforce
404 *bind* ed. (build Qq). Brown points out that 'build' is not meaningful, whereas
bind is in keeping with the associations of ll. 391–400 (p. 37).
407 *blind* i.e. like the Goddess Fortune
412 *humorous* ill humoured; crochety
413 The friends Alexander and Lodowick were so alike that they could change
places without anyone noticing. When Lodowick married the Princess of
Hungaria in Alexander's name, he laid a naked sword between the Princess
and himself each night so that his friend would not be wronged.
415 *shroud* veil
  3 *main* end, purpose

BOSOLA   Let me see, you have a reasonable good face for't
already, and your nightcap expresses your ears sufficient   5
largely; I would have you learn to twirl the strings of your
band with a good grace; and in a set speech, at th' end of
every sentence, to hum, three or four times, or blow your
nose, till it smart again, to recover your memory. When
you come to be a president in criminal causes, if you smile   10
upon a prisoner, hang him, but if you frown upon him, and
threaten him, let him be sure to scape the gallows.
CASTRUCHIO   I would be a very merry president, –
BOSOLA   Do not sup a nights; 'twill beget you an admirable
wit.   15
CASTRUCHIO   Rather it would make me have a good stomach
to quarrel, for they say your roaring boys eat meat seldom,
and that makes them so valiant: but how shall I know
whether the people take me for an eminent fellow?
BOSOLA   I will teach a trick to know it: give out you lie a-   20
dying, and if you hear the common people curse you, be
sure you are taken for one of the prime nightcaps.

[Enter OLD LADY]

You come from painting now?
OLD LADY   From what?
BOSOLA   Why, from your scurvy face physic: To behold   25
thee not painted inclines somewhat near a miracle. These
in thy face here, were deep ruts and foul sloughs, the last
progress. There was a lady in France, that having had the
smallpox, flayed the skin off her face, to make it more level;
and whereas before she look'd like a nutmeg grater, after   30
she resembled an abortive hedgehog.
OLD LADY   Do you call this painting?
BOSOLA   No, no but careening of an old morphew'd lady,

---

5 *nightcap* white coif worn by sergeants at law
  expresses presses out
6–7 *strings of your band* white tabs worn by sergeants
10 *president* presiding magistrate
17 *roaring boys* riotous bullies
22 *nightcaps* lawyers
23–43 Bosola's sentiments are anticipated in Justiniano's conversation with
  Birdlime in Dekker and Webster's *Westward Ho!* I.i.113–22 (Bowers II, p.
  322).
27 *sloughs* muddy ditches; layers of dead tissue
28 *progress* state journey
33 *No, no, but* McIlwraith, Brown (No, no but you call Qq 1–2; No, no but
  you call it Q3; No, no but [I] call [it] Lucas)
  careening scraping the paint off   *morphew'd* scurfy

to make her disembogue again. There's roughcast phrase
to your plaster.   35
⌐OLD LADY   It seems you are well acquainted with my
  closet?
BOSOLA   One would suspect it for a shop of witchcraft,
  to find in it the fat of serpents; spawn of snakes, Jews'
  spittle, and their young children's ordure, and all these for   40
  the face. I would sooner eat a dead pigeon, taken from the soles   misog
  of the feet of one sick of the plague, than kiss one of you
  fasting. Here are two of you, whose sin of your youth is the
  very patrimony of the physician, makes him renew his
  footcloth with the spring, and change his high-priz'd   45
  courtesan with the fall of the leaf: I do wonder you do not
  loathe yourselves. Observe my meditation now:
  What thing is in this outward form of man
  To be belov'd? We account it ominous,
  If nature do produce a colt, or lamb,   50
  A fawn, or goat, in any limb resembling
  A man; and fly from't as a prodigy.
  Man stands amaz'd to see his deformity,
  In any other creature but himself.
  But in our own flesh, though we bear diseases   55
  Which have their true names only tane from beasts,
  As the most ulcerous wolf, and swinish measle;
  Though we are eaten up of lice, and worms,
  And though continually we bear about us
  A rotten and dead body, we delight   60
  To hide it in rich tissue: all our fear,
  Nay, all our terror, is lest our physician
  Should put us in the ground, to be made sweet.

34 *disembogue* come out into the open sea
34–35 *There's ... plaster* i.e. 'There's the rough cast surface underneath your
    smoothly plastered exterior'. Read this way, Bosola's image is parallel to his
    previous one which implies that the Old Lady is an old battleship being
    made to look like a new one in preparation for war on the high seas.
35 *plaster* this edn (plastic Qq)
40 *children's ordure* Qq2–3 (children ordures Q1; Q4 *omits*)
42–43 i.e. 'when *you* are fasting and the offensiveness is therefore at its worst'
    (Lucas)
45 *footcloth* ornamental cloth covering a horse's back and hanging down to the
    ground. It protected the rider from mud and dust and was consequently a
    mark of dignity and status.
57 *ulcerous wolf* punning on the Latin word lupus = ulcer
    swinish measle Measle(s), applied to a skin disease in swine, was confused
    with ordinary measles.

Your wife's gone to Rome: you two couple, and get you
To the wells at Lucca, to recover your aches.   65

[*Exeunt* CASTRUCHIO *and* OLD LADY]

I have other work on foot: I observe our Duchess
Is sick a-days, she pukes, her stomach seethes,
The fins of her eyelids look most teeming blue,
She wanes i'th' cheek, and waxes fat i'th' flank;
And, contrary to our Italian fashion,   70
Wears a loose-bodied gown: there's somewhat in't.
I have a trick, may chance discover it,
A pretty one; I have bought some apricocks,
The first our spring yields.

[*Enter* ANTONIO *and* DELIO]

DELIO   And so long since married?
You amaze me.

ANTONIO   Let me seal your lips for ever,   75
For did I think that anything but th' air
Could carry these words from you, I should wish
You had no breath at all. [*To* BOSOLA] Now sir, in your
                                                  contemplation?
You are studying to become a great wise fellow?

BOSOLA   Oh sir, the opinion of wisdom is a foul tetter,   80
that runs all over a man's body: if simplicity direct us to
have no evil, it directs us to a happy being. For the subtlest
folly proceeds from the subtlest wisdom. Let me be simply
honest.

ANTONIO
I do understand your inside.   85

BOSOLA
Do you so?

65 *Lucca* a spa 13 miles N.E. of Pisa. Cf. III.ii.313.
66–74 In 'Science and Religion in John Webster's *The Duchess of Malfi*', *Studia
     Neophilologica* 49 (1977), 233–42, Marianne Nordfors describes the
     Duchess as 'probably the most realistically pregnant heroine ever put on
     the English stage. Bosola's description reads like a physician's journal ...
     In southern countries apricots, especially unripe ones, are known to purge.'
     Thus, as labour is known to be induced by a strong laxative, Bosola's
     apricots 'form an efficient if rather radical diagnostic instrument' (pp. 235–
     36).
67 *seethes* is inwardly agitated
68 *fins* rims
   teeming pregnant
73 *apricocks* apricots
80 *tetter* Q4 (tettor Qq1–2; terror Q3) skin eruption

ANTONIO

    Because you would not seem to appear to th' world
    Puff'd up with your preferment, you continue
    This out of fashion melancholy; leave it, leave it.

BOSOLA   Give me leave to be honest in any phrase, in any   90
    compliment whatsoever: shall I confess myself to you? I
    look no higher than I can reach: they are the gods, that
    must ride on winged horses, a lawyer's mule of a slow pace
    will both suit my disposition and business. For, mark me,
    when a man's mind rides faster than his horse can gallop   95
    they quickly both tire.

ANTONIO

    You would look up to Heaven, but I think
    The devil, that rules i'th' air, stands in your light.

BOSOLA   Oh, sir, you are lord of the ascendant, chief man
    with the Duchess: a duke was your cousin-german,   100
    remov'd. Say you were lineally descended from King
    Pippin, or he himself, what of this? Search the heads of the
    greatest rivers in the world, you shall find them but bubbles
    of water. Some would think the souls of princes were
    brought forth by some more weighty cause, than those of   105
    meaner persons; they are deceiv'd, there's the same hand to
    them: the like passions sway them; the same reason, that
    makes a vicar go to law for a tithe-pig, and undo his neigh-
    bours, makes them spoil a whole province, and batter down
    goodly cities with the cannon.   110

[Enter DUCHESS, OLD LADY, LADIES]

DUCHESS

    Your arm Antonio, do I not grow fat?
    I am exceeding short-winded. Bosola,
    I would have you, sir, provide for me a litter,
    Such a one, as the Duchess of Florence rode in.

---

  89 *of fashion* Qq2–4 (off shashion Q1)

  99 *lord of the ascendant* in astronomy, the ruling planet or dominating influence

100 *cousin-german* first cousin

101–2 *King Pippin* The last of the three Carolingian monarchs of this name (d.
    768) was the best known. His coronation, performed by St Boniface, was
    a ceremony new to France. At the request of Pope Stephen II he made
    expeditions to Italy in 754 and 756. By wresting the exarchate of Ravenna
    from Aistulf, King of the Lombards, and conferring it on the Pope, Pippin
    III became the veritable creator of the papal state. At his death his kingdom
    was divided between his sons Charles (Charlemagne) and Carloman.

108 *go* Q1 (to go Qq2–4)

BOSOLA

    The duchess us'd one, when she was great with child.   115

DUCHESS

    I think she did. Come hither, mend my ruff,

    Here; when? thou art such a tedious lady; and

    Thy breath smells of lemon peels; would thou hadst done;

    Shall I sound under thy fingers? I am

    So troubled with the mother.

BOSOLA [*Aside*]   I fear too much.   120

DUCHESS

    I have heard you say that the French courtiers

    Wear their hats on 'fore the king.

ANTONIO   I have seen it.

DUCHESS

    In the presence?

ANTONIO   Yes:

DUCHESS

    Why should not we bring up that fashion?

    'Tis ceremony more than duty, that consists   125

    In the removing of a piece of felt:

    Be you the example to the rest o'th' court,

    Put on your hat first.

ANTONIO   You must pardon me:

    I have seen, in colder countries than in France,

    Nobles stand bare to th' prince; and the distinction   130

    Methought show'd reverently.

BOSOLA

    I have a present for your Grace.

DUCHESS   For me sir?

BOSOLA

    Apricocks, Madam.

DUCHESS   O sir, where are they?

    I have heard of none to-year.

---

117 *when?* an exclamation of impatience

118 *peels* ed. (pils Qq1–2; pills Q3; pills Q4). Sampson pointed out that the Q1
    spelling could indicate either 'pills' or 'peels' and Lucas confirmed that the
    reference here is to peel.

119 *sound* Q1 (swound Qq2–4) swoon

120 *mother* hysterical passion characterized by a sense of swelling and suffocation
    too Qq2–4 (to Q1)

121 *courtiers* Qq2–4 (courties Q1)

122 *'fore* ed. (fore Qq1–2; before Qq3–4)

124 s.p. Q4 (Qq1–3 continue as Antonio's speech)

130 *bare* bare-headed

131 *Methought* Q4 (My thought Qq1–3)

134 *to-year* this year. Cf. to-day.

BOSOLA

    [*Aside*] Good, her colour rises.   135

DUCHESS

    Indeed I thank you: they are wondrous fair ones.

    What an unskilful fellow is our gardener!

    We shall have none this month.

BOSOLA

    Will not your Grace pare them?

DUCHESS

    No, they taste of musk, methinks; indeed they do.   140

BOSOLA

    I know not: yet I wish your Grace had par'd 'em.

DUCHESS

    Why?

BOSOLA I forgot to tell you the knave gard'ner,

    Only to raise his profit by them the sooner,

    Did ripen them in horse-dung.

DUCHESS   Oh you jest.

    [*To* ANTONIO] You shall judge: pray taste one.

ANTONIO   Indeed Madam,   145

    I do not love the fruit.

DUCHESS   Sir, you are loth

    To rob us of our dainties: 'tis a delicate fruit,

    They say they are restorative?

BOSOLA   'Tis a pretty art,

    This grafting.

DUCHESS   'Tis so: a bett'ring of nature.

BOSOLA

    To make a pippin grow upon a crab,   150

    A damson on a black-thorn: [*Aside*] How greedily she eats

                                   them!

    A whirlwind strike off these bawd farthingales,

    For, but for that, and the loose-bodied gown,

    I should have discover'd apparently

    The young springal cutting a caper in her belly.   155

DUCHESS

    I thank you, Bosola: they were right good ones,

149 *grafting* a *double entendre*

    a bett'ring of ed. (a bettring of Q1; bettring of Q2; bettering of Q3; bettering

    the Q4)

150 *a pippin* Q1 (pippin Qq2–3; Pippins Q4)

    crab crab-apple tree

152 *farthingales* hooped petticoats

154 *apparently* manifestly, openly

155 *springal* stripling

If they do not make me sick.

ANTONIO   How now Madam?

DUCHESS

This green fruit: and my stomach are not friends.
How they swell me!

BOSOLA

[*Aside*] Nay, you are too much swell'd already.   160

DUCHESS

Oh, I am in an extreme cold sweat.

BOSOLA   I am very sorry.   [*Exit*]

DUCHESS

Lights to my chamber! O, good Antonio,
I fear I am undone.   *Exit* DUCHESS.

DELIO   Lights there, lights!

ANTONIO

O my most trusty Delio, we are lost:
I fear she's fall'n in labour: and there's left   165
No time for her remove.

DELIO   Have you prepar'd
Those ladies to attend her? and procur'd
That politic safe conveyance for the midwife
Your duchess plotted?

ANTONIO   I have.

DELIO

Make use then of this forc'd occasion: 170
Give out that Bosola hath poison'd her,
With these apricocks: that will give some colour
For her keeping close.

ANTONIO   Fie, fie, the physicians
Will then flock to her.

DELIO   For that you may pretend
She'll use some prepar'd antidote of her own,   175
Lest the physicians should repoison her.

ANTONIO

I am lost in amazement: I know not what to think on't.

                    Ex[*eunt*].

164 *most trusty* Q1 (trusty Qq2–3; Dear Friend Q4)
168 *politic* cunning
     the midwife probably the Old Lady, who reappears in the following scene.
     In the 1980 MRE production she also appeared as a waiting woman. Her
     grotesquely made-up face, serving as a reminder of the corruption of the
     flesh and possibly also of the court, had a particular impact in juxtaposition
     with the youth and beauty of the Duchess's children, who were on stage at
     the beginning of III.ii.
173 *close* shut up from observation

Scene ii

[*Enter* BOSOLA *and* OLD LADY]

BOSOLA   So, so: there's no question but her tetchiness and
  most vulturous eating of the apricocks, are apparent signs
  of breeding, now?

OLD LADY   I am in haste, sir.

BOSOLA   There was a young waiting-woman, had a   5
  monstrous desire to see the glass-house –

OLD LADY   Nay, pray let me go:

BOSOLA   And it was only to know what strange instrument
  it was, should swell up a glass to the fashion of a woman's
  belly.   10

OLD LADY   I will hear no more of the glass-house, you are
  still abusing women!

BOSOLA   Who, I? no, only, by the way now and then,
  mention your frailties. The orange tree bears ripe and
  green fruit and blossoms altogether. And some of you give   15
  entertainment for pure love: but more, for more precious
  reward. The lusty spring smells well: but drooping autumn
  tastes well. If we have the same golden showers, that rained
  in the time of Jupiter the Thunderer: you have the same
  Danaes still, to hold up their laps to receive them: didst   20
  thou never study the mathematics?

OLD LADY   What's that, sir?

BOSOLA   Why, to know the trick how to make a many lines
  meet in one centre. Go, go; give your foster-daughters good
  counsel: tell them, that the devil takes delight to hang at a   25
  woman's girdle, like a false rusty watch, that she cannot
  discern how the time passes.   [*Exit* OLD LADY]

[*Enter* ANTONIO, DELIO, RODERIGO, GRISOLAN]

1–3 Bosola's lines could be soliloquy, with the Old Lady entering at 'breeding'
  as Dyce, Hazlitt, Vaughan and Brown indicate. Lucas makes ll. 1–3 an aside,
  with Bosola turning to the Old Lady at 'now?'. Sampson suggests that
  Bosola might be trying to gain information from her, and with this I concur.

1 *tetchiness* ed. irritability (teatchiues Q1; teatchives Qq2–3; eager Q4)

2 *apparent* obvious

6 *glass-house* glass factory. There was a famous one near the Blackfriars
  Theatre.

12 *still* always

14 *bears* Qq3–4 (beare Qq1–2)

18–20 Since Jupiter came to Danae in a golden shower, she was considered
  the type of mercenary woman. Cf. I.ii.168–69.

20 *Danaes* ed. (Danes Qq1–2; Dames Q3; Danae's Q4)

ANTONIO

    Shut up the court gates.

RODERIGO   Why sir? what's the danger?

ANTONIO

    Shut up the posterns presently: and call

    All the officers o'th' court.

GRISOLAN   I shall instantly.   [*Exit*]   30

ANTONIO

    Who keeps the key o'th' park-gate?

RODERIGO   Forobosco.

ANTONIO

    Let him bring't presently.   [*Exit* RODERIGO]

      [*Enter* SERVANTS, GRISOLAN, RODERIGO]

1 SERVANT

    Oh, gentlemen o'th' court, the foulest treason!

BOSOLA

    [*Aside*] If that these apricocks should be poison'd, now;

    Without my knowledge!

1 SERVANT   There was taken even now   35

    A Switzer in the Duchess' bedchamber.

2 SERVANT   A Switzer?

1 SERVANT

    With a pistol in his great cod-piece.

BOSOLA   Ha, ha, ha.

1 SERVANT

    The cod-piece was the case for't.

2 SERVANT   There was a cunning traitor.

    Who would have search'd his cod-piece?

1 SERVANT

    True, if he had kept out of the ladies' chambers: 40

    And all the moulds of his buttons were leaden bullets.

2 SERVANT

    Oh wicked cannibal: a fire-lock in's cod-piece?

---

28 *Shut* Qq2–4 (Shht Q1) Cf. l.37 below.

29 *presently* immediately

36 *a Switzer* a Swiss mercenary, such as were employed in feuds among the Italian nobility

37 *pistol* 'The current pronunciation of "pistol", without the "t", accentuates a pun on "pizzle" = penis' (Gunby).

    cod-piece a necessary appendage to the close-fitting hose or breeches of 15th to 17th centuries. Sometimes used as pockets, they were often ornamented: cf. *The White Devil* V.iii.98–101.

    Ha, ha, ha Qq2–4 (Hh, ha, ha Q1)

42 *cannibal* bloodthirsty savage

1 SERVANT
'Twas a French plot upon my life.
2 SERVANT   To see what the devil can do.
ANTONIO
All the officers here?
SERVANTS   We are.
ANTONIO   Gentlemen,
We have lost much plate you know; and but this evening   45
Jewels, to the value of four thousand ducats
Are missing in the Duchess' cabinet.
Are the gates shut?
1 SERVANT   Yes.
ANTONIO   'Tis the Duchess' pleasure
Each officer be lock'd into his chamber
Till the sun-rising; and to send the keys   50
Of all their chests, and of their outward doors
Into her bedchamber. She is very sick.
RODERIGO
At her pleasure.
ANTONIO
She entreats you take't not ill. The innocent
Shall be the more approv'd by it.   55
BOSOLA
Gentleman o'th' wood-yard, where's your Switzer now?
1 SERVANT   By this hand 'twas credibly reported by one
o'th' black-guard.
                 [*Exeunt* BOSOLA, RODERIGO *and* SERVANTS]
DELIO
How fares it with the Duchess?
ANTONIO   She's expos'd
Unto the worst of torture, pain, and fear.   60
DELIO
Speak to her all happy comfort.
ANTONIO
How I do play the fool with mine own danger!
You are this night, dear friend, to post to Rome,
My life lies in your service.
DELIO   Do not doubt me.

44 *officers* Qq2–4 (offices Q1)
47 *cabinet* private apartment, boudoir   55 *approv'd* commended
56 *Gentleman o'th' wood-yard* The First Servant had addressed the company as
    'gentlemen o'th' court' (l.33). In a *wood-yard* wood was stored or chopped,
    especially for fuel, so Bosola is mocking him for demeaning himself by his
    susceptibility to rumour which, as ll.57–58 confirm, originated below stairs.
57 *credibly* Q2, Q4 (creadably Q1; credibily Q2)
58 *black-guard* meanest drudges; scullions and turnspits

ANTONIO

 Oh, 'tis far from me: and yet fear presents me   65
 Somewhat that looks like danger.
DELIO   Believe it,
 'Tis but the shadow of your fear, no more:
 How superstitiously we mind our evils!
 The throwing down salt, or crossing of a hare;
 Bleeding at nose, the stumbling of a horse: 70
 Or singing of a cricket, are of power
 To daunt whole man in us. Sir, fare you well:
 I wish you all the joys of a bless'd father;
 And, for my faith, lay this unto your breast,
 Old friends, like old swords, still are trusted best. 75

           [*Exit* DELIO]

    [*Enter* CARIOLA *with a child*]

CARIOLA

 Sir, you are the happy father of a son,
 Your wife commends him to you.
ANTONIO   Blessed comfort!
 For heaven' sake tend her well: I'll presently
 Go set a figure for's nativity.   *Exeunt.*

Scene iii

   [*Enter* BOSOLA *with a dark lanthorn*]

BOSOLA

 Sure I did hear a woman shriek: list, ha?
 And the sound came, if I receiv'd it right,
 From the Duchess' lodgings: there's some stratagem
 In the confining all our courtiers
 To their several wards. I must have part of it,   5
 My intelligence will freeze else. List again,

66 *looks* Qq2–4 (looke Q1)
72 *whole man* completeness, self-reliance. Cf. *The White Devil* I.i.44.
74 *unto* Q1 (into Qq2–3; Q4 *omits*)
75 *Enter* CARIOLA *with a child* Q4
79 *figure* horoscope
Act II, Scene iii Stage directions are supplied from Q4.
 1 s.d. *dark lanthorn* a lantern with a slide or other arrangement whereby its
  light may be concealed. Cf. V.iv.42.
 5 *wards* apartments
 6 *intelligence* conveying secret information

It may be 'twas the melancholy bird,
Best friend of silence, and of solitariness,
The owl, that scream'd so: ha! Antonio?

[*Enter* ANTONIO *with a candle, his sword drawn*]

ANTONIO
I heard some noise: who's there? What art thou? Speak.   10
BOSOLA
Antonio! Put not your face nor body
To such a forc'd expression of fear,
I am Bosola; your friend.
ANTONIO   Bosola!
[*Aside*] This mole does undermine me – heard you not
A noise even now?
BOSOLA   From whence?
ANTONIO   From the Duchess' lodging.   15
BOSOLA
Not I: did you?
ANTONIO   I did: or else I dream'd.
BOSOLA
Let's walk towards it.
ANTONIO   No. It may be 'twas
But the rising of the wind.
BOSOLA   Very likely.
Methinks 'tis very cold, and yet you sweat.
You look wildly.
ANTONIO   I have been setting a figure   20
For the Duchess' jewels.
BOSOLA   Ah: and how falls your question?
Do you find it radical?
ANTONIO   What's that to you?
'Tis rather to be question'd what design,
When all men were commanded to their lodgings,
Makes you a night-walker.
BOSOLA   In sooth I'll tell you: 25
Now all the court's asleep, I thought the devil
Had least to do here; I come to say my prayers,
And if it do offend you, I do so,
You are a fine courtier.
ANTONIO [*Aside*]   This fellow will undo me.

9 *scream'd* ed. (schream'd Qq)   10 *who's* Qq3–4 (whose Qq1–2)
20–21 On the use of horoscopes for catching thieves and finding stolen goods, with particular reference to this passage, see Johnstone Parr, *Tamburlaine's Malady and Other Essays on Astrology in Elizabethan Drama* (University, Alabama; University of Alabama Press, 1953), pp. 101–6.
22 *radical* fit to be judged

You gave the Duchess apricocks to-day,   30
Pray heaven they were not poison'd!
BOSOLA   Poison'd! a Spanish fig
For the imputation.
ANTONIO   Traitors are ever confident,
Till they are discover'd. There were jewels stol'n too,
In my conceit, none are to be suspected
More than yourself.
BOSOLA   You are a false steward.   35
ANTONIO
Saucy slave! I'll pull thee up by the roots.
BOSOLA
May be the ruin will crush you to pieces.
ANTONIO
You are an impudent snake indeed, sir,
Are you scarce warm, and do you show your sting?
BOSOLA
. . .
ANTONIO
You libel well, sir.
BOSOLA   No sir, copy it out: 40
And I will set my hand to't.
ANTONIO   My nose bleeds.
One that were superstitious, would count
This ominous: when it merely comes by chance.
Two letters, that are wrought here for my name
Are drown'd in blood!   45
Mere accident: for you, sir, I'll take order:
I'th' morn you shall be safe: [*Aside*] 'tis that must colour
Her lying-in: sir, this door you pass not:
I do not hold it fit, that you come near

---

31 *Spanish fig* a term of contempt, accompanied by an indecent gesture
34 *conceit* opinion
38–46 This passage, on Sig. E₂ of Q1, was set up by Compositor A who, of the
    two working on the text, was the more likely to make errors in lineation, of
    which two occur between ll.41 and 46. The s.p. *Ant.* at ll.38 and 40 suggests
    the loss of something from Bosola, since ll.40–41 apparently refer to his
    willingness to sign a copy of the horoscope as proof of his desire to catch
    the thief and thus establish his own innocence. Obviously Antonio would
    be taking a risk in letting Bosola have sight of the child's horoscope: hence
    the irony of his dropping it when fumbling for a handkerchief to stanch his
    nose-bleed.
40 s.p. ANTONIO Ant. Q1 (Qq2–4 *omit*)
44 *wrought* Qq1–2 (wrote Qq3–4, Dyce, Hazlitt, Vaughan, McIlwraith) em-
    broidered. Had the letters been written (i.e. on the horoscope), Bosola
    would have been able to identify the child's father at once.

The Duchess' lodgings, till you have quit yourself;   50
[Aside] The great are like the base; nay, they are the same,
When they seek shameful ways to avoid shame.   *Ex[it].*
BOSOLA

Antonio here about did drop a paper,
Some of your help, false friend: oh, here it is.
What's here? a child's nativity calculated?   55
[Reads] The Duchess was deliver'd of a son, 'tween the hours
twelve and one, in the night: Anno Dom: 1504. (that's this
year) decimo nono Decembris, *(that's this night) taken*
according to the Meridian of Malfi (that's our Duchess: happy
discovery). The Lord of the first house, being combust in the   60
ascendant, signifies short life: and Mars being in a human
sign, join'd to the tail of the Dragon, in the eight house, doth
threaten a violent death; Cætera non scrutantur.
Why now 'tis most apparent. This precise fellow
Is the Duchess' bawd: I have it to my wish.   65
This is a parcel of intelligency
Our courtiers were cas'd up for! It needs must follow,
That I must be committed, on pretence
Of poisoning her: which I'll endure, and laugh at.
If one could find the father now: but that   70
Time will discover. Old Castruchio
I'th' morning posts to Rome; by him I'll send
A letter, that shall make her brother's galls
O'erflow their livers. This was a thrifty way.
Though lust do masque in ne'er so strange disguise   75
She's oft found witty, but is never wise.   *[Exit]*

50 *quit* Qq3–4 (quite Qq1–2)

54 *false friend* i.e. the dark lanthorn

56–63 For comment on this horoscope see Parr, *Tamburlaine's Malady*, pp. 94–100, Lucas II, p. 153 and Brown, p. 57. Parr thinks it indicates the futility of Delio's hope of establishing Antonio's son in his mother's right. The details of the horoscope indicate disaster, but these configurations did not occur at any time at the opening of the sixteenth century. As Antonio Bologna did not return to Naples from France till early 1505, December 1505 should perhaps be the date here: see Boklund, *Sources, Themes, Characters*, p. 4.

63 *Caetera non scrutantur* Qq2–4 (Caeteta non scrutantur Q1) 'the rest is not examined'

67 *cas'd* Qq2–4 (caside Q1) shut up. Cf. III.ii.139.

75 *masque* take part in a masque
   ne'er ed. (nea'r Qq1–2; ne're Qq 3–4)

Scene iv

[*Enter* CARDINAL *and* JULIA]

CARDINAL
  Sit: thou art my best of wishes; prithee tell me
  What trick didst thou invent to come to Rome,
  Without thy husband?
JULIA   Why, my Lord, I told him
  I came to visit an old anchorite
  Here, for devotion.
CARDINAL   Thou art a witty false one: 5
  I mean to him.
JULIA   You have prevailed with me
  Beyond my strongest thoughts: I would not now
  Find you inconstant.
CARDINAL   Do not put thyself
  To such a voluntary torture, which proceeds
  Out of your own guilt.
JULIA   How, my Lord?
CARDINAL   You fear   10
  My constancy, because you have approv'd
  Those giddy and wild turnings in yourself.
JULIA
  Did you e'er find them?
CARDINAL   Sooth, generally for women;
  A man might strive to make glass malleable,
  Ere he should make them fixed.
JULIA   So, my Lord.   15

Act II, Scene iv This scene, which, like the following one, is set in Rome, opens
with tension and dramatic irony, as we know that Castruchio is on his way
thither. Orazio Busino seems to have seen Julia on the Cardinal's knee (see Introduction, p. xxxiii.). In 'Webster and the Actor', *John Webster*, edited by Brian
Morris, Mermaid Critical Commentaries, Peter Thomson reports a suggestion
that the Cardinal's opening lines 'should be spoken post-coitally by a man who
has pushed through the business of the meeting before getting down to the small
talk' (pp. 32–33). This was realized by BBC television in 1972 and the MRE in
1980. In the 1989/90 RSC production Julia entered centre stage, raising her
skirts by degrees as she moved downstage to obey the Cardinal's command by
sitting astride a chair with her legs fully displayed.

  5 *Here* Qq2–4 (Heare Q1)
    5, 24 *witty* and *wisely* emphasize that Julia and the Cardinal embody Bosola's
      sententious conclusion to the previous scene.
  12 *turnings* Qq3–4 (turning Qq1–2)

CARDINAL

We had need go borrow that fantastic glass
Invented by Galileo the Florentine,
To view another spacious world i'th' moon,
And look to find a constant woman there.

JULIA

This is very well, my Lord.

CARDINAL   Why do you weep?   20
Are tears your justification? The selfsame tears
Will fall into your husband's bosom, lady,
With a loud protestation that you love him
Above the world. Come, I'll love you wisely,
That's jealously, since I am very certain   25
You cannot me make cuckold.

JULIA   I'll go home
To my husband.

CARDINAL   You may thank me, lady,
I have taken you off your melancholy perch,
Bore you upon my fist, and show'd you game,
And let you fly at it. I pray thee kiss me.   30
When thou wast with thy husband, thou wast watch'd
Like a tame elephant: (still you are to thank me.)
Thou hadst only kisses from him, and high feeding,
But what delight was that? 'Twas just like one
That hath a little fing'ring on the lute,   35
Yet cannot tune it: (still you are to thank me.)

JULIA

You told me of a piteous wound i'th' heart,
And a sick liver, when you wooed me first,
And spake like one in physic.

CARDINAL   Who's that?

[*Enter* SERVANT]

Rest firm, for my affection to thee,   40
Lightning moves slow to't.

SERVANT   Madam, a gentleman

16–19 This is an anachronistic reference to the telescope constructed by Galileo
    in 1609 after he had heard of the one made by the Dutch spectacle-maker
    Nippershay.
25 *That's* Qq1–2 (That Qq3–4)
26 *me make* Q1 (make me Q2, Q4; make me a Q3)
28–30 The Cardinal speaks as if Julia were a falcon.
30 *pray thee* ed. (pray the Q1; prethee Qq2–3; prithee Q4)
33–36 The *double entendre* here indicates both the Cardinal's corruption and
    his spiritual kinship with Ferdinand.
39 *in physic* under medical surveillance   41 *to't* in comparison to it

That's come post from Malfi, desires to see you.
CARDINAL
  Let him enter, I'll withdraw.   *Exit*.
SERVANT   He says
  Your husband, old Castruchio, is come to Rome,
  Most pitifully tir'd with riding post.   [*Exit* SERVANT]   45

[*Enter* DELIO]

JULIA
  Signior Delio! [*Aside*] 'tis one of my old suitors.
DELIO
  I was bold to come and see you.
JULIA   Sir, you are welcome.
DELIO
  Do you lie here?
JULIA   Sure, your own experience
  Will satisfy you no; our Roman prelates
  Do not keep lodging for ladies.
DELIO   Very well.   50
  I have brought you no commendations from your husband,
  For I know none by him.
JULIA   I hear he's come to Rome?
DELIO
  I never knew man and beast, of a horse and a knight,
  So weary of each other; if he had had a good back,
  He would have undertook to have borne his horse,   55
  His breach was so pitifully sore.
JULIA   Your laughter
  Is my pity.
DELIO   Lady, I know not whether
  You want money, but I have brought you some.
JULIA
  From my husband?
DELIO   No, from mine own allowance.
JULIA
  I must hear the condition, ere I be bound to take it.   60
DELIO
  Look on't, 'tis gold, hath it not a fine colour?

45 *tir'd* Q4 (tyr'd Qq1–3)
47 *to come and* Q1 (and come to Qq2–3; Q4 *changes sense*)
49 *no* Q1, Q4 (now Qq2–3)
56–57 Julia teasingly equivocates with Delio so that he does not know whether
    she pities her husband's impotence or merely deplores its effect on herself.
59 *mine* Qq1–2 (my Qq3–4)

JULIA
I have a bird more beautiful.
DELIO   Try the sound on't.
JULIA
A lute-string far exceeds it;
It hath no smell, like cassia or civet,
Nor is it physical, though some fond doctors   65
Persuade us, seethe't in cullises. I'll tell you,
This is a creature bred by –

[*Enter* SERVANT]

SERVANT   Your husband's come,
Hath deliver'd a letter to the Duke of Calabria,
That, to my thinking, hath put him out of his wits.
                                              [*Exit* SERVANT]
JULIA
Sir, you hear,   70
Pray let me know your business and your suit,
As briefly as can be.
DELIO   With good speed. I would wish you,
At such time, as you are non-resident
With your husband, my mistress.
JULIA
Sir, I'll go ask my husband if I shall,   75
And straight return your answer.   *Exit.*
DELIO   Very fine,
Is this her wit, or honesty that speaks thus?
I heard one say the Duke was highly mov'd
With a letter sent from Malfi. I do fear
Antonio is betray'd: how fearfully   80
Shows his ambition now; unfortunate Fortune!
They pass through whirlpools, and deep woes do shun,
Who the event weigh, ere the action's done.   *Exit.*

---

64 *cassia* coarser kind of cinnamon
    civet perfume with a strong musky smell
65 *physical* medicinal
66 *seethe't* Dyce (seeth's Qq 1–2; seeth'd Q3; Q4 *changes sense*)
    cullises strengthening broths, made by bruising meat
77 *honesty* honour in the sense of chastity
    speaks Q1 (speak Qq2–4)

Scene v

[Enter] CARDINAL, *and* FERDINAND, *with a letter.*

FERDINAND
  I have this night digg'd up a mandrake.
CARDINAL   Say you?
FERDINAND
  And I am grown mad with't.
CARDINAL   What's the prodigy?
FERDINAND
  Read there, a sister damn'd, she's loose, i'th' hilts:
  Grown a notorious strumpet.
CARDINAL   Speak lower.
FERDINAND   Lower?
  Rogues do not whisper't now, but seek to publish't,   5
  As servants do the bounty of their lords,
  Aloud; and with a covetous searching eye,
  To mark who note them. Oh confusion seize her,
  She hath had most cunning bawds to serve her turn,
  And more secure conveyances for lust,   10
  Than towns of garrison, for service.
CARDINAL   Is't possible?
  Can this be certain?
FERDINAND   Rhubarb, oh for rhubarb
  To purge this choler; here's the cursed day
  To prompt my memory, and here't shall stick
  Till of her bleeding heart I make a sponge   15
  To wipe it out.

---

  1 s.d. Qq 1–3 (*Cardinal and Ferdinand, Furious, with a Letter* Q4)
  1 *digg'd* ed. (Q1a dig; Q1b dig'd)
    say you? what do you say?
  1–2 The mandrake, a plant of the genus Mandragora, has a forked root and
    thus resembles the human form. Supposed to grow under the gallows, it
    was said to shriek when pulled from the ground and plucking it would lead
    to madness.
  2 *prodigy* ed. (progedy Qq1–2; prodegy Qq3–4)
  3 *damn'd* Qq2–4 (dampn'd Q1)
    loose, i'th' hilts unreliable, like the loose handle of a dagger or sword (used
    here in the sense of unchaste)
  10 *secure conveyances* safe passages
  11 *service* military service; sexual intercourse
  12–13 *rhubarb* Considered to be choleric itself, rhubarb was a recognized
    antidote for an excess of choler.
  13 *the cursed day* i.e. in the horoscope, which Bosola has sent with his letter
  14 *here't* Qq2–4 (here'it Q1)

CARDINAL   Why do you make yourself
  So wild a tempest?
FERDINAND   Would I could be one,
  That I might toss her palace 'bout her ears,
  Root up her goodly forests, blast her meads,
  And lay her general territory as waste,   20
  As she hath done her honour's.
CARDINAL   Shall our blood?
  The royal blood of Aragon and Castile,
  Be thus attainted?
FERDINAND   Apply desperate physic,
  We must not now use balsamum, but fire,
  The smarting cupping-glass, for that's the mean   25
  To purge infected blood, such blood as hers.
  There is a kind of pity in mine eye,
  I'll give it to my handkercher; and now 'tis here,
  I'll bequeath this to her bastard.
CARDINAL   What to do?
FERDINAND
  Why, to make soft lint for his mother's wounds,   30
  When I have hewed her to pieces.
CARDINAL   Curs'd creature!
  Unequal nature, to place women's hearts
  So far upon the left side.
FERDINAND   Foolish men,
  That e'er will trust their honour in a bark,
  Made of so slight, weak bulrush, as is woman,   35
  Apt every minute to sink it!

21 *honour's* ed. (honours Qq1–2, Sampson, Lucas; honours Qq3–4, Dyce, Hazlitt, Vaughan, McIlwraith, Brown). The honour to which Ferdinand refers is his sister's chastity and reputation for chastity, the damage to which extends to affect her whole family. Honour in this sense is uncountable. Thus the phrase means 'as she has done the general territory of her honour' i.e. her own and her family's.

24 *balsamum* aromatic healing ointment

28 *handkercher* Qq1–2 (handkerchief Qq3–4)

30 *mother's wounds* Q4 (mother wounds Q1; mothers wounds Qq2–3)

32 *unequal* unjust, partial

33 *left side* the wrong side. Dent quotes Matthieu's *History of Lewis the Eleventh* (1614) – 'The hearts of men lie on the left side, they are full of deceit, Truth freedome and loyalty are rare, vnknowne and exiled qualities' – commenting that the 'margin indicates Matthieu is being both literal and figurative' (p. 201). 'Left' in the sense of 'wrong' is found in the Ulster phrase, 'He digs with the left foot': i.e. 'He is of the wrong [religious] persuasion.' Cf. III.i.29n.

35 *is* Q1 (this Qq2–4)

CARDINAL
  Thus ignorance, when it hath purchas'd honour,
  It cannot wield it.
FERDINAND   Methinks I see her laughing,
  Excellent hyena! Talk to me somewhat, quickly,
  Or my imagination will carry me   40
  To see her in the shameful act of sin.
CARDINAL
  With whom?
FERDINAND
  Happily, with some strong thigh'd bargeman;
  Or one o'th' wood-yard, that can quoit the sledge
  Or toss the bar, or else some lovely squire   45
  That carries coals up to her privy lodgings.
CARDINAL
  You fly beyond your reason.
FERDINAND   Go to, mistress!
  'Tis not your whore's milk, that shall quench my wild-fire
  But your whore's blood.
CARDINAL
  How idly shows this rage! which carries you,   50
  As men convey'd by witches, through the air
  On violent whirlwinds: this intemperate noise
  Fitly resembles deaf men's shrill discourse,
  Who talk aloud, thinking all other men
  To have their imperfection.
FERDINAND   Have not you   55
  My palsy?
CARDINAL   Yes, I can be angry
  Without this rupture; there is not in nature
  A thing, that makes man so deform'd, so beastly
  As doth intemperate anger; chide yourself:
  You have divers men, who never yet express'd   60

37 *purchas'd* obtained
43 *Happily* haply, maybe
44 *wood-yard* Cf. II.ii.56n.
    quoit the sledge throw the sledge-hammer
46 *privy* Q1 (*private* Qq2–3; Q4 *omits*)
47 *Go to* an expression of disapprobation; also, go to it!
48 *shall* Q1 (*can* Qq2–4)
    wild-fire furious and destructive fire, easily ignited and difficult to extinguish;
    eruptive skin disease in children
56 *Yes, I* Qq, Sampson (Yes; I Hazlitt; Yes – I Lucas, Brown; Yes [but]
    I Dyce, Vaughan; Yes, yet I Brereton, McIlwraith)
57 *rupture* Qq (rapture conj. Dyce)

Their strong desire of rest but by unrest,
By vexing of themselves. Come, put yourself
In tune.
FERDINAND   So, I will only study to seem
The thing I am not. I could kill her now,
In you, or in myself, for I do think   65
It is some sin in us, Heaven doth revenge
By her.
CARDINAL   Are you stark mad?
FERDINAND   I would have their bodies
Burnt in a coal-pit, with the ventage stopp'd,
That their curs'd smoke might not ascend to Heaven:
Or dip the sheets they lie in, in pitch or sulphur,   70
Wrap them in't, and then light them like a match:
Or else to boil their bastard to a cullis,
And give't his lecherous father, to renew
The sin of his back.
CARDINAL   I'll leave you.
FERDINAND   Nay, I have done;
I am confident, had I been damn'd in hell,   75
And should have heard of this, it would have put me
Into a cold sweat. In, in, I'll go sleep:
Till I know who leaps my sister, I'll not stir:
That known, I'll find scorpions to string my whips,
And fix her in a general eclipse.   *Exeunt.*   80

Act III, Scene i

[*Enter* ANTONIO *and* DELIO]

ANTONIO

Our noble friend, my most beloved Delio,
Oh, you have been a stranger long at court,
Came you along with the Lord Ferdinand?

DELIO

I did, sir, and how fares your noble Duchess?

ANTONIO

Right fortunately well. She's an excellent   5

66 See III.v. 79–80n.
68 *coal-pit* a pit in which charcoal is made
72 *cullis* See II.iv.66n.
79 *string* Q1 (sting Qq2–4)
80 *general eclipse* total eclipse
Act III, Scenes i & ii These scenes take place in the Duchess's palace at Amalfi.

Feeder of pedigrees: since you last saw her,
She hath had two children more, a son and daughter.
DELIO
Methinks 'twas yesterday. Let me but wink,
And not behold your face, which to mine eye
Is somewhat leaner: verily I should dream   10
It were within this half hour.
ANTONIO
You have not been in law, friend Delio,
Nor in prison, nor a suitor at the court,
Nor begg'd the reversion of some great man's place,
Nor troubled with an old wife, which doth make   15
Your time so insensibly hasten.
DELIO   Pray sir tell me,
Hath not this news arriv'd yet to the ear
Of the Lord Cardinal?
ANTONIO   I fear it hath;
The Lord Ferdinand, that's newly come to court,
Doth bear himself right dangerously.
DELIO   Pray why?   20
ANTONIO
He is so quiet, that he seems to sleep
The tempest out, as dormice do in winter;
Those houses, that are haunted, are most still,
Till the devil be up.
DELIO   What say the common people?
ANTONIO
The common rabble do directly say   25
She is a strumpet.
DELIO   And your graver heads,
Which would be politic, what censure they?
ANTONIO
They do observe I grow to infinite purchase
The left-hand way, and all suppose the Duchess

6–8 'The time gap between this scene and the remainder of the action led the
   RSC [then the Stratford-on-Avon Company] 1960 production to put the
   interval here' (McLuskie and Uglow, p. 117). Productions which do not
   follow this example do Webster a disservice by rendering these lines unin-
   tentionally farcical. The 1985 NT production omitted these children: see
   'The Actors' Names', 16n (p. 2).
8 *wink* close the eyes. Cf. I.ii.268.
27 *be* Qq2–4 (he Q1)
   censure form an opinion
28 *purchase* acquired wealth
29 *left-hand* sinister

Would amend it, if she could. For, say they,   30
Great princes, though they grudge their officers
Should have such large and unconfined means
To get wealth under them, will not complain
Lest thereby they should make them odious
Unto the people: for other obligation   35
Of love, or marriage, between her and me,
They never dream of.

[*Enter* FERDINAND, DUCHESS *and* BOSOLA]

DELIO   The Lord Ferdinand
  Is going to bed.
FERDINAND   I'll instantly to bed,
  For I am weary: I am to bespeak
  A husband for you.
DUCHESS   For me, sir! pray who is't?   40
FERDINAND
  The great Count Malateste.
DUCHESS   Fie upon him,
  A count? He's a mere stick of sugar-candy,
  You may look quite thorough him: when I choose
  A husband, I will marry for your honour.
FERDINAND
  You shall do well in't. How is't, worthy Antonio?   45
DUCHESS
  But, sir, I am to have private conference with you,
  About a scandalous report is spread
  Touching mine honour.
FERDINAND   Let me be ever deaf to't:
  One of Pasquil's paper bullets, court calumny,

31–35 From John Donne, *Ignatius his Conclave* (1611): '... *Princes* who though
  they enuy and grudge, that their great Officers should have such immoderate
  meanes to get wealth; yet they dare not complaine of it, least thereby they
  should make them odious and contemptible to the people' (Dent, p. 203).
37 *of* Qq2–4 (off Q1)
39 *to* Qq2–4 (to be Q1)
42–43 Webster repeated the comment verbatim in *The Devil's Law-Case*
  II.i.138–40: '... you are a mere stick of sugar candy; a man may look quite
  thorough you.' Cf. Ben Jonson, *Cynthia's Revels* V.iv. 108–10: 'He is a mere
  peece of glasse, I see through him, by this time' (H & S II, p. 142).
48 *mine* Qq1–2 (my Qq3–4)
49 *Pasquil's paper bullets* Pasquil was a schoolmaster (or perhaps a cobbler) in
  fifteenth-century Rome with a bitter tongue. His name was given to a statue
  in the Piazza Narvona to which satirical verses and lampoons, known as
  pasquinades, were attached by the citizens for amusement. The original
  pasquinades were published in 1544. They were particularly in vogue in
  Italy 1585–90.

A pestilent air, which princes' palaces   50
Are seldom purg'd of. Yet, say that it were true,
I pour it in your bosom, my fix'd love
Would strongly excuse, extenuate, nay deny
Faults were they apparent in you. Go, be safe
In your own innocency.
DUCHESS   Oh bless'd comfort,   55
This deadly air is purg'd.   *Exeunt* [DUCHESS, ANTONIO, DELIO]
FERDINAND   Her guilt treads on
Hot burning cultures. Now Bosola,
How thrives our intelligence?
BOSOLA   Sir, uncertainly:
'Tis rumour'd she hath had three bastards, but
By whom, we may go read i'th' stars.
FERDINAND   Why some   60
Hold opinion, all things are written there.
BOSOLA
Yes, if we could find spectacles to read them;
I do suspect, there hath been some sorcery
Us'd on the Duchess.
FERDINAND   Sorcery, to what purpose?
BOSOLA
To make her dote on some desertless fellow,   65
She shames to acknowledge.
FERDINAND   Can your faith give way
To think there's power in potions, or in charms,
To make us love, whether we will or no?
BOSOLA
Most certainly.
FERDINAND
Away, these are mere gulleries, horrid things   70
Invented by some cheating mountebanks
To abuse us. Do you think that herbs, or charms
Can force the will? Some trials have been made
In the foolish practice; but the ingredients

---

51 *of* ed. (off Qq1–3; Q4 *omits*)
54 *were* Q3 (where Qq1–2; Q4 *omits*)
57 *cultures* coulters, plough-shares. The ability to tread on red-hot coulters
    (usually nine) was deemed, in Anglo-Saxon law, to vindicate a woman
    accused of unchastity. Among other ladies, Emma, the mother of Edward
    the Confessor, submitted to this test and thereby established her innocence.
66–78 See Additional Notes, p. 135.
70 *horrid* Qq3–4 (horred Qq1–2)

Were lenative poisons, such as are of force   75
To make the patient mad; and straight the witch
Swears, by equivocation, they are in love.
The witchcraft lies in her rank blood: this night
I will force confession from her. You told me
You had got, within these two days, a false key   80
Into her bed-chamber.
BOSOLA   I have.
FERDINAND   As I would wish.
BOSOLA
  What do you intend to do?
FERDINAND   Can you guess?
BOSOLA   No.
FERDINAND
  Do not ask then.
  He that can compass me, and know my drifts,
  May say he hath put a girdle 'bout the world,   85
  And sounded all her quick-sands.
BOSOLA   I do not
  Think so.
FERDINAND   What do you think then? pray?
BOSOLA   That you
  Are your own chronicle too much: and grossly
  Flatter yourself.
FERDINAND   Give me thy hand; I thank thee.
  I never gave pension but to flatterers,   90
  Till I entertained thee: farewell,
  That friend a great man's ruin strongly checks,
  Who rails into his belief all his defects.   *Exeunt.*

---

75 *lenative poisons* bawdy aphrodisiacs. Lucas's guess that lenative comes from
    '*lenare* to prostitute' is confirmed by the context of Webster's borrowing.
    Cf. 66–78n, p. 135.
77 *by equivocation,* Q4 (by equivocation; Qq1–2; (by equivocation) Q3)
78 *blood* Qq2–4 (bood Q1)
87 *then? pray?* Q1 (then, pray? Qq2–4)

Scene ii

[*Enter* DUCHESS, ANTONIO *and* CARIOLA]

DUCHESS
  Bring me the casket hither, and the glass;
  You get no lodging here to-night, my lord.
ANTONIO
  Indeed, I must persuade one.
DUCHESS   Very good:
  I hope in time 'twill grow into a custom,
  That noblemen shall come with cap and knee,   5
  To purchase a night's lodging of their wives.
ANTONIO
  I must lie here.
DUCHESS   Must? you are a lord of mis-rule.
ANTONIO
  Indeed, my rule is only in the night.
DUCHESS
  To what use will you put me?
ANTONIO   We'll sleep together.
DUCHESS
  Alas, what pleasure can two lovers find in sleep?   10
CARIOLA
  My lord, I lie with her often: and I know
  She'll much disquiet you.
ANTONIO   See, you are complain'd of.
CARIOLA
  For she's the sprawling'st bedfellow.
ANTONIO
  I shall like her the better for that.

Scene ii Though in 1960 and 1971 the RSC presented this scene austerely – see
McLuskie and Uglow, p. 123 – the precarious nature of the private life of the
Duchess and Antonio has also been emphasized through the stage presence of
their children. In the 1980 MRE production they were seen playing happily in
the care of the Old Lady (cf. II.i.168n.). In the 1989/90 RSC production the
placing and moving of necessary props was combined with the removal of
evidence of the children's presence, the last piece of which – a toy horse – was
nervously held by Cariola, whose tension was heightened by the off-stage cry of
a child. The toy provided a metaphor for family life under threat, but the stage
business raised irrelevant questions about the nature and extent of the courtiers'
knowledge of and complicity in maintaining the Duchess's domestic life.
    5 *with cap and knee* with cap in hand and bended knee: i.e. humbly
    7 *lord of mis-rule* (1) master of the revels (which took place at night); (2) lord
      of the rule of mistresses

CARIOLA

Sir, shall I ask you a question?   15

ANTONIO

I pray thee Cariola.

CARIOLA

Wherefore still, when you lie with my lady
Do you rise so early?

ANTONIO   Labouring men,
Count the clock oft'nest Cariola,
Are glad when their task's ended.

DUCHESS   I'll stop your mouth. [*Kisses him*]   20

ANTONIO

Nay, that's but one, Venus had two soft doves
To draw her chariot: I must have another. [*Kisses her*]
When wilt thou marry, Cariola?

CARIOLA   Never, my lord.

ANTONIO

O fie upon this single life: forgo it.
We read how Daphne, for her peevish flight   25
Became a fruitless bay-tree; Sirinx turn'd
To the pale empty reed; Anaxarete
Was frozen into marble: whereas those
Which married, or prov'd kind unto their friends
Were, by a gracious influence, transhap'd   30
Into the olive, pomegranate, mulberry:
Became flowers, precious stones, or eminent stars.

CARIOLA

This is vain poetry: but I pray you tell me,
If there were propos'd me wisdom, riches, and beauty,
In three several young men, which should I choose?   35

ANTONIO

'Tis a hard question. This was Paris' case
And he was blind in't, and there was great cause:
For how wasn't possible he could judge right,
Having three amorous goddesses in view,

---

16 *I* Qq (Ay   Dyce, Hazlitt, Vaughan, McIlwraith)
25 *peevish* perverse
    flight Dyce (slight Qq)
26 *Sirinx* Q4 (Sirina Q1a; Siriux Q1b–Q3)
27 *Anaxarete* ed. (Anaxorate Q1a; Anaxarate Q1b–Q4)
25–40 McLuskie and Uglow note that, in the 1980 MRE production the
    Duchess removed her very elaborate jewellery throughout Antonio's badi-
    nage with Cariola, thus achieving 'the difficult balance between the Duchess'
    femininity and her dignity' (p. 125).
38 *could* Q1 (should Qq2–4)

And they stark naked? 'Twas a motion   40
Were able to benight the apprehension
Of the severest counsellor of Europe.
Now I look on both your faces, so well form'd
It puts me in mind of a question, I would ask.
CARIOLA
What is't?
ANTONIO   I do wonder why hard favour'd ladies   45
For the most part, keep worse-favour'd waiting-women,
To attend them, and cannot endure fair ones.
DUCHESS
Oh, that's soon answer'd.
Did you ever in your life know an ill painter
Desire to have his dwelling next door to the shop   50
Of an excellent picture-maker? 'Twould disgrace
His face-making, and undo him. I prithee
When were we so merry? My hair tangles.
ANTONIO
[*Aside* to CARIOLA] Pray thee, Cariola, let's steal forth
                                              the room,
And let her talk to herself: I have divers times   55
Serv'd her the like, when she hath chaf'd extremely.
I love to see her angry: softly Cariola.
                              Exeunt [ANTONIO *and* CARIOLA].
DUCHESS
Doth not the colour of my hair 'gin to change?
When I wax grey, I shall have all the court
Powder their hair with arras, to be like me: 60
You have cause to love me, I ent'red you into my heart.

                  [*Enter* FERDINAND, *unseen*]

Before you would vouchsafe to call for the keys.
We shall one day have my brothers take you napping.
Methinks his presence, being now in court,
Should make you keep your own bed: but you'll say   65

---

40 *motion* display
41 *apprehension* Qq2–3 (approbation Q1a; apprehention Q1b; Q4 *omits*)
46 *waiting* Qq3–4 (wai-ting Q1a; waieting Q1b; wayting Q2)
50 *his* Q1b (the Q1a)
53 *so* Q1 (Qq2–4 *omit*)
56 *hath* Q1 (has Qq2–4)
60 *arras* the white powder of orris-root, smelling of violets
61 s.d. Q4 (*not in* Qq1–3). See III.ii.146n.
   I enter'd you Q1 (I enter'd Qq2–3; it enter'd Q4)

Love mix'd with fear is sweetest. I'll assure you
You shall get no more children till my brothers
Consent to be your gossips. Have you lost your tongue?

[*She sees* FERDINAND *holding a poniard*]

'Tis welcome:
For know, whether I am doom'd to live, or die,   70
I can do both like a prince.

FERDINAND *gives her a poniard.*

FERDINAND   Die then, quickly.
Virtue, where art thou hid? What hideous thing
Is it, that doth eclipse thee?
DUCHESS   Pray sir hear me –
FERDINAND
Or is it true, thou art but a bare name,
And no essential thing?
DUCHESS   Sir –
FERDINAND   Do not speak.   75
DUCHESS
No sir:
I will plant my soul in mine ears, to hear you.
FERDINAND
Oh most imperfect light of human reason,
That mak'st us so unhappy, to foresee
What we can least prevent. Pursue thy wishes: 80
And glory in them: there's in shame no comfort,
But to be past all bounds and sense of shame.
DUCHESS
I pray sir, hear me: I am married –
FERDINAND   So.
DUCHESS
Happily, not to your liking: but for that

---

68 *your gossips* godparents of your child
69 The Duchess may catch sight of Ferdinand in the mirror as she brushes her
   hair: see George Rylands, 'On the Production of *The Duchess of Malfi*',
   Sylvan Press edition of the play (London, 1945), p. ix. Potter, in 'Realism
   versus Nightmare,' develops both this idea and that of Antonio's speech to
   Cariola in relation to other of the play's reflections and metamorphoses (pp.
   184–85).
71 s.d. Q1b margin, opposite the two parts of line 71 (*not in* Q1a)
73 *eclipse* Q4 (ecclipze Q1; clip Qq2–3)
78 *most* Q1 (must Qq2–4)
79 *mak'st us* Q4 (mak'st Qq1–3)
84 *Happily* haply, perhaps

Alas: your shears do come untimely now   85
To clip the bird's wings, that's already flown.
Will you see my husband?
FERDINAND   Yes, if I could change
Eyes with a basilisk.
DUCHESS   Sure, you came hither
By his confederacy.
FERDINAND   The howling of a wolf
Is music to thee, screech-owl; prithee peace.   90
Whate'er thou art, that hast enjoy'd my sister,
(For I am sure thou hear'st me), for thine own sake
Let me not know thee. I came hither prepar'd
To work thy discovery: yet am now persuaded
It would beget such violent effects   95
As would damn us both. I would not for ten millions
I had beheld thee; therefore use all means
I never may have knowledge of thy name;
Enjoy thy lust still, and a wretched life,
On that condition. And for thee, vild woman,   100
If thou do wish thy lecher may grow old
In thy embracements, I would have thee build
Such a room for him, as our anchorites
To holier use inhabit. Let not the sun
Shine on him, till he's dead. Let dogs and monkeys   105
Only converse with him, and such dumb things
To whom nature denies use to sound his name.
Do not keep a paraquito, lest she learn it;
If thou do love him, cut out thine own tongue
Lest it bewray him.
DUCHESS   Why might not I marry?   110
I have not gone about, in this, to create
Any new world, or custom.

---

88 *basilisk* Both breath and sight of this fabulous creature were supposed to
    have power to kill.
89 *confederacy* Qq3–4 (consideracy Qq1–2)
90 *to thee* Q4 (to the Qq1–3) compared to thee
92 *hear'st* Q4 (hearst Q1; heardst Qq2–3)
    thine Q1, Q4 (mine Qq2–3)
95 *such* Q1 (so Qq2–4)
96 *damn* Qq3–4 (dampe Q1; damne Q2)
100 *vild* Q1 (vilde) vile (wilde Q2; wild Q3; vile Q4)
107ˇ *use to* ability to
110 *bewray* Qq1–3 (betray Q4)
110–12 See Additional Notes, p. 135.

FERDINAND   Thou art undone:
  And thou hast tane that massy sheet of lead
  That hid thy husband's bones, and folded it
  About my heart.
DUCHESS   Mine bleeds for't.
FERDINAND   Thine? thy heart?   115
  What should I name't, unless a hollow bullet
  Fill'd with unquenchable wild-fire?
DUCHESS   You are in this
  Too strict: and were you not my princely brother
  I would say too wilful. My reputation
  Is safe.
FERDINAND   Dost thou know what reputation is?   120
  I'll tell thee, to small purpose, since th'instruction
  Comes now too late:
  Upon a time Reputation, Love and Death
  Would travel o'er the world: and it was concluded
  That they should part, and take three several ways.   125
  Death told them, they should find him in great battles:
  Or cities plagu'd with plagues. Love gives them counsel
  To inquire for him 'mongst unambitious shepherds,
  Where dowries were not talk'd of: and sometimes
  'Mongst quiet kindred, that had nothing left   130
  By their dead parents. 'Stay', quoth Reputation,
  'Do not forsake me: for it is my nature
  If once I part from any man I meet
  I am never found again.' And so, for you:
  You have shook hands with Reputation,   135
  And made him invisible. So fare you well.
  I will never see you more.
DUCHESS   Why should only I,
  Of all the other princes of the world
  Be cas'd up, like a holy relic? I have youth,
  And a little beauty.
FERDINAND   So you have some virgins,   140
  That are witches. I will never see thee more.   *Exit.*

        Enter [CARIOLA *and*] ANTONIO *with a pistol.*

---

113 *ta'en* ed. (ta'ne Q1a, Qq3–4; taine Q1b–c, Q2)
    massy Qq2–4 (massiy Q1)
116 *hollow bullet* cannon ball
117 *wild-fire.* See II.v.48n.
118 *too* Qq2–4 (to Q1)
124 *it* Q1b–c, Qq2–4 (lt Q1a)
135 *shook* Qq3–4 (shooked Q1a–b; shooke Q1c–Q2)

DUCHESS
  You saw this apparition?
ANTONIO   Yes: we are
  Betray'd; how came he hither? I should turn
  This, to thee, for that. [*Points the pistol at* CARIOLA]
CARIOLA   Pray sir do: and when
  That you have cleft my heart, you shall read there,   145
  Mine innocence.
DUCHESS   That gallery gave him entrance.
ANTONIO
  I would this terrible thing would come again,
  That, standing on my guard, I might relate
  My warrantable love. *She shows the poniard.* Ha! what means
                                            this?
DUCHESS
  He left this with me.
ANTONIO   And it seems, did wish   150
  You would use it on yourself?
DUCHESS   His action seem'd
  To intend so much.
ANTONIO   This hath a handle to't,
  As well as a point: turn it towards him, and
  So fasten the keen edge in his rank gall. [*Knocking*]
  How now? Who knocks? More earthquakes?
DUCHESS   I stand   155
  As if a mine, beneath my feet, were ready
  To be blown up.
CARIOLA   'Tis Bosola.
DUCHESS   Away!
  Oh misery, methinks unjust actions
  Should wear these masks and curtains; and not we.
  You must instantly part hence: I have fashion'd it already.   160
                                    Ex[*it*] ANT[ONIO]

                            [*Enter* BOSOLA]

BOSOLA
  The Duke your brother is tane up in a whirlwind;
  Hath took horse, and's rid post to Rome.

---

146 *That gallery* Lucas wondered if Ferdinand is 'meant to be visible to the
    audience while crossing the upper stage, before he actually appears in the
    Duchess's room' (Lucas II, 165). I think he is, thus creating great tension
    for the scene – similar to that of II.iv – and underlining the parallel between
    the Duchess and Julia.
149 s.d. is placed to the right of the two lines of type which constitute l. 150 in
    Q1.

DUCHESS   So late?

BOSOLA

He told me, as he mounted into th' saddle,
You were undone.

DUCHESS   Indeed, I am very near it.   165

BOSOLA

What's the matter?

DUCHESS   Antonio, the master of our household
Hath dealt so falsely with me, in's accounts:
My brother stood engag'd with me for money
Tane up of certain Neapolitan Jews,
And Antonio lets the bonds be forfeit.   170

BOSOLA

Strange: [*Aside*] this is cunning.

DUCHESS   And hereupon
My brother's bills at Naples are protested
Against. Call up our officers.

BOSOLA   I shall.   *Exit.*

[*Enter* ANTONIO]

DUCHESS

The place that you must fly to, is Ancona,
Hire a house there. I'll send after you   175
My treasure, and my jewels: our weak safety
Runs upon enginous wheels: short syllables
Must stand for periods. I must now accuse you
Of such a feigned crime, as Tasso calls
Magnanima mensogna: a noble lie,   180
'Cause it must shield our honours: hark, they are coming.

[*Enter* BOSOLA *and* OFFICERS]

ANTONIO

Will your Grace hear me?

DUCHESS

I have got well by you: you have yielded me

---

167 *in's* in his   170 *lets* Q4 (let's Qq1–3)
173 *our* Q1 (the Qq2–4)   176 *jewels* ed. (Iewlls Q1; Jewels Qq2–4)
177 *enginous* ed. (engeneous Q1; ingenious Qq2–4); *enginous wheels* wheels like
     those of a clock whose small, almost imperceptible movement produces
     obvious motion of the hands
180 *Magnanima mensogna* alludes to Tasso's *Gerusalemne Liberata* II, xxii where
     a Christian maiden falsely admits to taking a statue of the Virgin Mary from
     a mosque, thereby saving her co-religionists from persecution.
183–93 The Duchess's equivocal language is both a statement of her trust in
     Antonio and an explicit reminder to him of her wooing. Cf. III.ii.187;
     I.ii.378–80.

A million of loss; I am like to inherit
The people's curses for your stewardship.   185
You had the trick, in audit time to be sick,
Till I had sign'd your *Quietus*; and that cur'd you
Without help of a doctor. Gentlemen,
I would have this man be an example to you all:
So shall you hold my favour. I pray let him;   190
For h'as done that, alas! you would not think of,
And, because I intend to be rid of him,
I mean not to publish. Use your fortune elsewhere.

ANTONIO

I am strongly arm'd to brook my overthrow,
As commonly men bear with a hard year: 195
I will not blame the cause on't; but do think
The necessity of my malevolent star
Procures this, not her humour. O the inconstant
And rotten ground of service, you may see;
'Tis ev'n like him that, in a winter night,   200
Takes a long slumber, o'er a dying fire
As loth to part from't: yet parts thence as cold,
As when he first sat down.

DUCHESS   We do confiscate,
Towards the satisfying of your accounts,
All that you have.

ANTONIO   I am all yours; and 'tis very fit   205
All mine should be so.

DUCHESS   So, sir; you have your pass.

ANTONIO

You may see, gentlemen, what 'tis to serve
A prince with body and soul.   *Exit.*

BOSOLA   Here's an example for extortion; what moisture is
drawn out of the sea, when foul weather comes, pours down,   210
and runs into the sea again.

DUCHESS

I would know what are your opinions
Of this Antonio.

2 OFFICER   He could not abide to see a pig's head gaping,
I thought your Grace would find him a Jew: 215

---

190 *let him* (1) let him go; (2) prevent him from going
191 *h'as* he has
202 *As loth* Q1c (A-loth Q1a–b)
203 *confiscate* Q1b–c (confifcate Q1a)
209 *extortion* Qq1–2 (exhortation Qq3–4)

3 OFFICER　I would you had been his officer, for your own
sake.

4 OFFICER　You would have had more money.

1 OFFICER　He stopp'd his ears with black wool: and to
those came to him for money said he was thick of hearing.　220

2 OFFICER　Some said he was an hermaphrodite, for he
could not abide a woman.

4 OFFICER.　How scurvy proud he would look, when the
treasury was full. Well, let him go.

1 OFFICER　Yes, and the chippings of the butt'ry fly after　225
him, to scour his gold chain.

DUCHESS

Leave us. What do you think of these?　　*Exeunt* [OFFICERS].

BOSOLA

That these are rogues, that in's prosperity,
But to have waited on his fortune, could have wish'd
His dirty stirrup riveted through their noses:　　　　　　230
And follow'd after's mule, like a bear in a ring.
Would have prostituted their daughters to his lust;
Made their first born intelligencers; thought none happy
But such as were born under his bless'd planet;
And wore his livery: and do these lice drop off now?　　235
Well, never look to have the like again;
He hath left a sort of flatt'ring rogues behind him,
Their doom must follow. Princes pay flatterers,
In their own money. Flatterers dissemble their vices,
And they dissemble their lies, that's justice.　　　　　　240
Alas, poor gentleman, –

216 *his* Q1 (Qq2–4 *omit*)
220 *those . . . money* enclosed in brackets in Q1a-b
223 *he would* Q1 (would he Qq2–4)
225 *chippings* parings of a crust of bread
226 *gold chain* Q1, Q4 (golden chain Qq2–3), the steward's badge of office
228ff. As McLuskie and Uglow point out, these lines are crucial for an actor's
　　　　and audience's understanding of Bosola's characterization: i.e. is his admir-
　　　　ation of Antonio genuine, or is this 'another of his elaborately cynical
　　　　deceptions?' (p. 135). Frank Whigham believes that it is both: 'Bosola's own
　　　　sincere response managed in pursuit of his employer's goal' ('Sexual and
　　　　Social Mobility', p. 179).
229 *his* Q1, Q4 (this Qq2–3)
231 *in a ring* with a ring through his nose
233 *intelligencers* Q1c (and Intelligencers Q1a-b)
234 *bless'd* Q1 (Qq2–4 *omit*)
235 *livery* Q1c (Liuory Qq1a-b)
237 *sort* collection
238 *doom* Qq3–4 (doombe Qq1a–b; doome Q1c–Q2)

DUCHESS

Poor! he hath amply fill'd his coffers.

BOSOLA

Sure he was too honest. Pluto the god of riches,
When he's sent, by Jupiter, to any man
He goes limping, to signify that wealth   245
That comes on God's name, comes slowly; but when he's
                                                               sent
On the devil's errand, he rides post, and comes in by
                                                            scuttles.
Let me show you what a most unvalu'd jewel
You have, in a wanton humour, thrown away.
To bless the man shall find him. He was an excellent   250
Courtier, and most faithful; a soldier, that thought it
As beastly to know his own value too little,
As devilish to acknowledge it too much;
Both his virtue and form deserv'd a far better fortune:
His discourse rather delighted to judge itself, than show
                                                            itself.   255
His breast was fill'd with all perfection,
And yet it seem'd a private whisp'ring room:
It made so little noise of't.

DUCHESS   But he was basely descended.

BOSOLA

Will you make yourself a mercenary herald,
Rather to examine men's pedigrees, than virtues?   260
You shall want him:
For know an honest statesman to a prince,
Is like a cedar, planted by a spring,
The spring bathes the tree's root, the grateful tree
Rewards it with his shadow: you have not done so;   265
I would sooner swim to the Bermoothas on
Two politicians' rotten bladders, tied
Together with an intelligencer's heart string

243 *Pluto*, the god of the underworld, was confused with Plutus, god of riches,
      probably through the idea of wealth coming from underground mines.
247 *On* Qq2–4 (One Q1)
      by scuttles scuttling
248 *unvalu'd* (1) invaluable; (2) undervalued
255 *discourse* conversational power
266 *Bermoothas* ed. (Bermoothes Q1a-b; Bermootha's Qq1c-3; Q4 *omits*)
      Bermudas. Famous for storms, these islands had attracted particular atten-
      tion after the shipwreck there of Sir George Summers, in 1609.
267 *politicians* crafty and intriguing schemers

Than depend on so changeable a prince's favour.
Fare thee well, Antonio, since the malice of the world   270
Would needs down with thee, it cannot be said yet
That any ill happened unto thee,
Considering thy fall was accomplished with virtue.

DUCHESS

Oh, you render me excellent music.

BOSOLA   Say you?

DUCHESS

This good one that you speak of, is my husband.   275

BOSOLA

Do I not dream? Can this ambitious age
Have so much goodness in't, as to prefer
A man merely for worth: without these shadows
Of wealth, and painted honours? possible?

DUCHESS

I have had three children by him.

BOSOLA   Fortunate lady,   280
For you have made your private nuptial bed
The humble and fair seminary of peace.
No question but many an unbenefic'd scholar
Shall pray for you, for this deed, and rejoice
That some preferment in the world can yet   285
Arise from merit. The virgins of your land,
That have no dowries, shall hope your example
Will raise them to rich husbands. Should you want
Soldiers, 'twould make the very Turks and Moors
Turn Christians, and serve you for this act.   290
Last, the neglected poets of your time,
In honour of this trophy of a man,
Rais'd by that curious engine, your white hand,
Shall thank you in your grave for't; and make that
More reverend than all the cabinets   295
Of living princes. For Antonio,
His fame shall likewise flow from many a pen,
When heralds shall want coats, to sell to men.

DUCHESS

As I taste comfort, in this friendly speech,
So would I find concealment –

BOSOLA   Oh the secret of my prince,   300

278 Q1 (Qq2–4 *omit*)
279 *painted* false, deceptive. Cf. IV.ii.330.
282 *seminary* nursery; seed-bed
298 *coats* coats of arms

Which I will wear on th'inside of my heart.

DUCHESS

You shall take charge of all my coin, and jewels,
And follow him, for he retires himself
To Ancona.

BOSOLA   So.

DUCHESS   Whither, within few days,
I mean to follow thee.

BOSOLA   Let me think: 305
I would wish your Grace to feign a pilgrimage
To Our Lady of Loretto, scarce seven leagues
From fair Ancona, so may you depart
Your country with more honour, and your flight
Will seem a princely progress, retaining   310
Your usual train about you.

DUCHESS   Sir, your direction
Shall lead me, by the hand.

CARIOLA   In my opinion,
She were better progress to the baths at Lucca,
Or go visit the Spa
In Germany: for, if you will believe me,   315
I do not like this jesting with religion,
This feigned pilgrimage.

DUCHESS   Thou art a superstitious fool:
Prepare us instantly for our departure.
Past sorrows, let us moderately lament them,
For those to come, seek wisely to prevent them.   320

Exit [DUCHESS *with* CARIOLA].

BOSOLA

A politician is the devil's quilted anvil,
He fashions all sins on him, and the blows
Are never heard; he may work in a lady's chamber,
As here for proof. What rests, but I reveal
All to my lord? Oh, this base quality   325
Of intelligencer! Why, every quality i'th' world
Prefers but gain, or commendation:
Now for this act, I am certain to be rais'd,
And men that paint weeds, to the life, are prais'd.   *Exit.*

---

304 *Whither* Qq3–4 (Whether Qq1–2)
313 *Lucca* See II.i.65n.
314 *Spa* was in Belgium but, to Webster's audience, all the Low Countries were
     alike 'Dutch' or 'German'.

Scene iii

[*Enter*] CARDINAL, FERDINAND, MALATESTE, PESCARA, SILVIO,
DELIO.

CARDINAL
  Must we turn soldier then?
MALATESTE   The Emperor,
  Hearing your worth that way, ere you attain'd
  This reverend garment, joins you in commission
  With the right fortunate soldier, the Marquis of Pescara
  And the famous Lannoy.
CARDINAL   He that had the honour   5
  Of taking the French king prisoner?
MALATESTE   The same.
  Here's a plot drawn for a new fortification
  At Naples.
FERDINAND   This great Count Malateste, I perceive
  Hath got employment.
DELIO   No employment, my lord,
  A marginal note in the muster book, that he is   10
  A voluntary lord.
FERDINAND   He's no soldier?
DELIO
  He has worn gunpowder, in's hollow tooth,
  For the tooth-ache.
SILVIO
  He comes to the leaguer with a full intent
  To eat fresh beef, and garlic; means to stay   15
  Till the scent be gone, and straight return to court.

Scene iii Lucas located the scene on the outer stage; the 1989/90 RSC production
on the upper stage. McLuskie and Uglow believe it takes place in the camp (p.
15). I think it unlikely that the Cardinal would visit the leaguer or receive visitors
there until he had divested himself of his ecclesiastical garments, and so I assume
that he is here visited by Malateste, Bosola and Ferdinand in his palace, in Rome.

  1 *The Emperor* Charles V
  4 *Marquis of Pescara* Ferdinando Francesco d'Avolos (1489–1525)
  5 *Lannoy* Charles de Lannoy, Viceroy of Naples (c. 1487–1527), to whom
    alone Francis I of France would surrender his sword at Pavia in 1525. The
    reference to the event here is obviously anachronistic.
  7 *plot* diagram
 14 *comes* Q1 (come Q2; came Q3; Q4 *omits*)
    leaguer military camp
 16 *be gone* Q3 (begon Q1; be gon Q2; Q4 *omits*)

DELIO
    He hath read all the late service,
    As the City chronicle relates it,
    And keeps two painters going, only to express
    Battles in model.
SILVIO   Then he'll fight by the book.   20
DELIO
    By the almanac, I think,
    To choose good days, and shun the critical.
    That's his mistress' scarf.
SILVIO   Yes, he protests
    He would do much for that taffeta, –
DELIO
    I think he would run away from a battle   25
    To save it from taking prisoner.
SILVIO   He is horribly afraid
    Gunpowder will spoil the perfume on't, –
DELIO
    I saw a Dutchman break his pate once
    For calling him pot-gun; he made his head
    Have a bore in't, like a musket.   30
SILVIO
    I would he had made a touch-hole to't.
    He is indeed a guarded sumpter-cloth
    Only for the remove of the court.

                  [*Enter* BOSOLA]

PESCARA
    Bosola arriv'd? What should be the business?
    Some falling out amongst the cardinals.   35
    These factions amongst great men, they are like
    Foxes, when their heads are divided:
    They carry fire in their tails, and all the country
    About them goes to wrack for't.

17 *service* military operations
19 *keeps* Qq2–3 (keepe Q1; Q4 *omits*)
    painters Q1c (pewterers Q1a-b)
20 *he'll* Qq2–3 (hel Q1; Q4 *omits*)
23 *critical* related to the crisis or turning-point; crucial
32 *guarded sumpter-cloth* decorated saddle cloth used on such special occasions
    as a royal progress
37–39 These lines allude to the story told in Judges 15. 4–5, of Samson's tying
    300 foxes together in pairs by their tails, attaching firebrands to them and
    letting them loose in the Philistines' standing corn, thereby destroying not
    only their grain, but their vines and olives as well.
39 *goes to wrack* is devastated (cf. 'goes to wrack and ruin')

SILVIO   What's that Bosola?
DELIO   I knew him in Padua, a fantastical scholar, like   40
    such who study to know how many knots was in Hercules'
    club; of what colour Achilles' beard was, or whether Hector
    were not troubled with the toothache. He hath studied
    himself half blear-ey'd, to know the true symmetry of
    Caesar's nose by a shoeing-horn: and this he did to gain the 45
    name of a speculative man.
PESCARA
    Mark Prince Ferdinand,
    A very salamander lives in's eye,
    To mock the eager violence of fire.
SILVIO   That cardinal hath made more bad faces with his   50
    oppression than ever Michael Angelo made good ones: he
    lifts up's nose, like a foul porpoise before a storm, –
PESCARA   The Lord Ferdinand laughs.
DELIO   Like a deadly cannon, that lightens ere it smokes.
PESCARA
    These are your true pangs of death,   55
    The pangs of life, that struggle with great statesmen, –
DELIO   In such a deformed silence, witches whisper their
    charms.
CARDINAL
    Doth she make religion her riding hood
    To keep her from the sun and tempest?
FERDINAND   That: 60
    That damns her. Methinks her fault and beauty
    Blended together, show like leprosy,
    The whiter, the fouler. I make it a question
    Whether her beggarly brats were ever christ'ned.
CARDINAL
    I will instantly solicit the state of Ancona   65
    To have them banish'd.
FERDINAND   You are for Loretto?
    I shall not be at your ceremony; fare you well:
    Write to the Duke of Malfi, my young nephew
    She had by her first husband, and acquaint him
    With's mother's honesty.
BOSOLA   I will.
FERDINAND   Antonio!   70
    A slave, that only smell'd of ink and counters,

65 *state* ruling authorities
69 *her first* Q1, Q3 (first Q2; Q4 *omits*)
71 *counters* small discs used for calculating

And nev'r in's life look'd like a gentleman,
But in the audit time: go, go presently,
Draw me out an hundred and fifty of our horse,
And meet me at the fort-bridge.   *Exeunt.*   75

Scene iv

[*Enter*] TWO PILGRIMS *to the Shrine of Our Lady of Loretto.*

1 PILGRIM
I have not seen a goodlier shrine than this,
Yet I have visited many.
2 PILGRIM   The Cardinal of Aragon
Is this day to resign his cardinal's hat;
His sister duchess likewise is arriv'd
To pay her vow of pilgrimage. I expect   5
A noble ceremony.
1 PILGRIM   No question. – They come.

*Here the ceremony of the Cardinal's instalment in the habit of a
soldier: perform'd in delivering up his cross, hat, robes, and ring
at the shrine; and investing him with sword, helmet, shield, and
spurs. Then* ANTONIO, *the* DUCHESS *and their children, having
presented themselves at the shrine, are (by a form of banishment
in dumb-show expressed towards them by the* CARDINAL, *and the
state of* ANCONA) *banished. During all which ceremony this Ditty
is sung to very solemn music, by divers churchmen; and then*
                                             Exeunt.

72 *life* Qq2–4 (like Q1)
74 *hundred* Qq2–4 (hundreth Q1)
Act III, Scenes iv and v These scenes take place in Loretto. Scene iv is omitted
entirely in Q4 as it has been in some modern productions, e.g. by the RSC at
the Barbican in London (1990), though it had been included at the Swan in
Stratford (1989), when the Cardinal had no hat to deliver up, as the directions
say he should. Webster's disclaiming authorship of the ditty suggests that the
King's Men had sought to enliven the scene, which attracted the attention of
Busino: see Introduction, p. xxxiii above.
  1 *shrine* Q1, Q3 (shrive Q2)
  6 s.d.: *habit* Q1b (order Q1a)
     of a Qq2–3 (a Q1)
     shrine Q1 (shrive Q2; shrieve Q3)
     banishment in dumb-show Q1b (banishment Q1a)
     Ditty Q1b (Hymn Q1a)
  7 [*untitled*] Q1b (The Hymne Q1a)

Arms and honours deck thy story,
To thy fame's eternal glory,
Adverse fortune ever fly thee,   The Au-
No disastrous fate come nigh thee.   thor dis-   10
I alone will sing thy praises,   claims
Whom to honour virtue raises;   this Ditty
And thy study that divine is,   to be his.
Bent to martial discipline is:
Lay aside all those robes lie by thee,   15
Crown thy arts with arms: they'll beautify thee.

O worthy of worthiest name, adorn'd in this manner,
Lead bravely thy forces on, under war's warlike banner:
O mayst thou prove fortunate in all martial courses,
Guide thou still by skill, in arts and forces: 20
Victory attend thee nigh, whilst fame sings loud thy powers,
Triumphant conquest crown thy head, and blessings pour down
                                              showers.

1 PILGRIM

Here's a strange turn of state: who would have thought
So great a lady would have match'd herself
Unto so mean a person? Yet the Cardinal   25
Bears himself much too cruel.

2 PILGRIM   They are banish'd.

1 PILGRIM

But I would ask what power hath this state
Of Ancona, to determine of a free prince?

2 PILGRIM

They are a free state sir, and her brother show'd
How that the Pope, forehearing of her looseness,   30
Hath seiz'd into th' protection of the Church
The dukedom which she held as dowager.

9–12 *The Au- … his.* Q1b (Q1a, Qq 2–3 *omit*)

9–14 In Q1 the last two words of ll. 9, 10, 13 and 14 are hyphenated, thus
  indicating the fall of stress.

26 *much too* Q1 (too Qq2–3)

28 *determine of* come to a judicial decision about

29 *free state* Ancona was, at this time, a semi-independent republic under papal
  protection.
  sir Q1b (Q1a *omits*)

31 *Hath* Q1b (Had Q1a)

1 PILGRIM
  But by what justice?
2 PILGRIM   Sure I think by none,
  Only her brother's instigation.
1 PILGRIM
  What was it, with such violence he took   35
  Off from her finger?
2 PILGRIM   'Twas her wedding-ring,
  Which he vow'd shortly he would sacrifice
  To his revenge.
1 PILGRIM   Alas Antonio!
  If that a man be thrust into a well,
  No matter who sets hand to't, his own weight   40
  Will bring him sooner to th' bottom. Come, let's hence.
  Fortune makes this conclusion general,
  All things do help th'unhappy man to fall.   *Exeunt.*

Scene v

[*Enter*] ANTONIO, DUCHESS, CHILDREN, CARIOLA, SERVANTS.

DUCHESS
  Banish'd Ancona?
ANTONIO   Yes, you see what power
  Lightens in great men's breath.
DUCHESS   Is all our train
  Shrunk to this poor remainder?
ANTONIO   These poor men,
  Which have got little in your service, vow
  To take your fortune. But your wiser buntings   5
  Now they are fledg'd are gone.
DUCHESS   They have done wisely;
  This puts me in mind of death: physicians thus,
  With their hands full of money, use to give o'er
  Their patients.
ANTONIO   Right the fashion of the world:

  34 *brother's* ed. (brothers Qq) i.e. the Cardinal's. Cf. III.iii.65–66.
  36 *off* Qq2–3 (of Q1)
    1 *Ancona?* Qq, Sampson, Gunby (Ancona! Dyce, Lucas, Brown) The form
      of Antonio's response and the Duchess's following query reinforce the
      impression that her opening words express bewilderment rather than violent
      emotion.
    3 *These* Q1 (These are Qq2–3)
    5 *buntings* small birds related to the lark family
    9 *Right* just

From decay'd fortunes every flatterer shrinks,   10
Men cease to build where the foundation sinks.

DUCHESS

I had a very strange dream tonight.

ANTONIO   What was't?

DUCHESS

Methought I wore my coronet of state,
And on a sudden all the diamonds
Were chang'd to pearls.

ANTONIO   My interpretation   15
Is, you'll weep shortly; for to me, the pearls
Do signify your tears.

DUCHESS   The birds, that live i'th' field
On the wild benefit of nature, live
Happier than we; for they may choose their mates,
And carol their sweet pleasures to the spring.   20

[*Enter* BOSOLA *with a letter which he presents to the* DUCHESS]

BOSOLA

You are happily o'ertane.

DUCHESS   From my brother?

BOSOLA

Yes, from the Lord Ferdinand; your brother,
All love, and safety –

DUCHESS   Thou dost blanch mischief;
Wouldst make it white. See, see; like to calm weather
At sea before a tempest, false hearts speak fair   25
To those they intend most mischief. [*She reads*] *A Letter*:
Send Antonio to me; I want his head in a business.
(A politic equivocation)
He doth not want your counsel, but your head;
That is, he cannot sleep till you be dead.   30
And here's another pitfall, that's strew'd o'er
With roses: mark it, 'tis a cunning one:
I stand engaged for your husband for several debts at Naples:

12 *was't* Q1, Q4 (is't Qq2–3)
18 *benefit* favour; gift
22 *Ferdinand; your* The semicolon implies a pause for 'there is indeed a distance
between Ferdinand and brotherliness' (Lucas II, 207).
24 *to* Q1, Q4 (to the Qq2–3)
28 *politic equivocation* cunning use of words of double meaning with intent to
deceive
33–39 Ferdinand's equivocation recalls the attitude of Shylock to Antonio's
bond (*The Merchant of Venice* IV.i.223–26). His letter uses the same excuse
to demand Antonio's presence that the Duchess gave for Antonio's dismissal:
cf. III.ii.166–70.

let not that trouble him, I had rather have his heart than his
money.   35
And I believe so too.
BOSOLA   What do you believe?
DUCHESS
  That he so much distrusts my husband's love,
  He will by no means believe his heart is with him
  Until he see it. The devil is not cunning enough
  To circumvent us in riddles.   40
BOSOLA
  Will you reject that noble and free league
  Of amity and love which I present you?
DUCHESS
  Their league is like that of some politic kings
  Only to make themselves of strength and power
  To be our after-ruin: tell them so.   45
BOSOLA
  And what from you?
ANTONIO   Thus tell them: I will not come.
BOSOLA
  And what of this?
ANTONIO   My brothers have dispers'd
  Bloodhounds abroad; which till I hear are muzzl'd
  No truce, though hatch'd with ne'er such politic skill
  Is safe, that hangs upon our enemies' will.   50
  I'll not come at them.
BOSOLA   This proclaims your breeding.
  Every small thing draws a base mind to fear;
  As the adamant draws iron: fare you well sir,
  You shall shortly hear from's.   *Exit.*
DUCHESS   I suspect some ambush:
  Therefore by all my love; I do conjure you   55
  To take your eldest son, and fly towards Milan;
  Let us not venture all this poor remainder
  In one unlucky bottom.
ANTONIO   You counsel safely.
  Best of my life, farewell. Since we must part
  Heaven hath a hand in't: but no otherwise   60
  Than as some curious artist takes in sunder
  A clock, or watch, when it is out of frame
  To bring't in better order.
DUCHESS   I know not which is best,

47 *brothers* i.e. brothers-in-law
53 *adamant* loadstone
58 *bottom* (hold of a) ship

To see you dead, or part with you. Farewell boy,
Thou art happy, that thou hast not understanding   65
To know thy misery. For all our wit
And reading brings us to a truer sense
Of sorrow. In the eternal Church, sir,
I do hope we shall not part thus.
ANTONIO   O be of comfort,
Make patience a noble fortitude: 70
And think not how unkindly we are us'd.
Man, like to cassia, is prov'd best being bruis'd.
DUCHESS
Must I like to a slave-born Russian,
Account it praise to suffer tyranny?
And yet, O Heaven, thy heavy hand is in't.   75
I have seen my little boy oft scourge his top,
And compar'd myself to't: nought made me e'er go right,
But Heaven's scourge-stick.
ANTONIO   Do not weep:
Heaven fashion'd us of nothing; and we strive
To bring ourselves to nothing. Farewell Cariola,   80
And thy sweet armful. [*To the* DUCHESS] If I do never see
                                                 thee more,
Be a good mother to your little ones,
And save them from the tiger: fare you well.
DUCHESS
Let me look upon you once more: for that speech
Came from a dying father: your kiss is colder   85
Than I have seen an holy anchorite
Give to a dead man's skull.

---

68 *the eternal Church* the Church triumphant
72 Quotation marks, indicating that the line is one of the play's *sententiae*,
  were omitted in Q1a: see Note on the Text, p. xxxix.
73 *Russian* Q1 (Ruffian Qq2–4)
78 *scourge-stick* whip for a top
79–80 Webster's source is Donne's *An Anatomy of the World: The First Anni-*
  versary, ll. 155–57:
      We seem ambitious, God's whole work to undo;
      Of nothing he made us, and we strive too,
      To bring ourselves to nothing back …
  The change from 'God' to 'Heaven' may have been necessitated by the
  requirements of the Lord Chamberlain, as G.P.V. Akrigg has suggested in
  'The Name of God and *The Duchess of Malfi*', *N&Q* 195 (1950), 231–33.
  Other substitutions of 'Heaven' for 'God' may be found at I.ii.393; II.v.66;
  III.v.75, 78; III.v.97; IV.ii.218; V.iii.40.

ANTONIO

My heart is turn'd to a heavy lump of lead,
With which I sound my danger: fare you well.

Exit [with elder SON].

DUCHESS

My laurel is all withered.   90

CARIOLA

Look, Madam, what a troop of armed men
Make toward us.

Enter BOSOLA *with a guard [vizarded].*

DUCHESS   O, they are very welcome:
When Fortune's wheel is over-charg'd with princes,
The weight makes it move swift. I would have my ruin
Be sudden. I am your adventure, am I not?   95

BOSOLA

You are: you must see your husband no more, –

DUCHESS

What devil art thou, that counterfeits Heaven's thunder?

BOSOLA

Is that terrible? I would have you tell me whether
Is that note worse that frights the silly birds
Out of the corn; or that which doth allure them   100
To the nets? You have heark'ned to the last too much.

DUCHESS

O misery! like to a rusty o'ercharg'd cannon,
Shall I never fly in pieces? Come: to what prison?

BOSOLA

To none.

DUCHESS   Whither then?

---

91 *what a* Q1b (what Q1a)
92 s.d. Q1b (Q1a *omits*)
94 *move* Q1b (*more* Q1a)
95 *adventure* quarry
98 s.p. *Bos.* Q1b (Q1a *omits*)
99 *silly* innocent
102 s.p. *Duch.* Q1b (Q1a *Ant.*)
     o'ercharg'd ed. (orechar'd Q1; ore-charg'd Qq2–3; Q4 *omits*)
102–3 Cf. John Donne, *Of the Progress of the Soul: The Second Anniversary*, ll.
     181–82:
        Think that a rustie piece, discharged is flown
        In pieces . . .
     and Dekker and Webster, *Northward Ho!* II.ii.136–39: 'if she hould pure
     mettaile two yeare and flie to seuerall peeces, in the third, repaire the ruines
     of her honesty at your charges, for the best peece of ordinance, may bee
     crackt in the casting . . .' (Bowers II, p. 437)

BOSOLA   To your palace.
DUCHESS
  I have heard that Charon's boat serves to convey   105
  All o'er the dismal lake, but brings none back again.
BOSOLA
  Your brothers mean you safety and pity.
DUCHESS
  Pity!
  With such a pity men preserve alive
  Pheasants and quails, when they are not fat enough   110
  To be eaten.
BOSOLA
  These are your children?
DUCHESS   Yes.
BOSOLA   Can they prattle?
DUCHESS
  No:
  But I intend, since they were born accurs'd;
  Curses shall be their first language.
BOSOLA   Fie, Madam!   115
  Forget this base, low fellow.
DUCHESS   Were I a man,
  I'll'd beat that counterfeit face into thy other –
BOSOLA
  One of no birth.
DUCHESS   Say that he was born mean,
  Man is most happy, when's own actions
  Be arguments and examples of his virtue.   120
BOSOLA
  A barren, beggarly virtue.
DUCHESS
  I prithee, who is greatest, can you tell?
  Sad tales befit my woe: I'll tell you one.
  A Salmon, as she swam unto the sea,
  Met with a Dog-fish; who encounters her   125
  With this rough language: 'Why art thou so bold
  To mix thyself with our high state of floods
  Being no eminent courtier, but one
  That for the calmest and fresh time o'th' year
  Dost live in shallow rivers, rank'st thyself   130

109 *such a* Q1b (such Q1a)
117 *counterfeit face* i.e. the vizard
122–38 Both compositors make frequent use of capitals. Here capitalization
    stresses the meaning of the Duchess's parable. It has, therefore, been
    preserved, except in sea, courtier and rivers. See Note on the Text, p. xxxix.

With silly Smelts and Shrimps? And darest thou
Pass by our Dog-ship without reverence?'
'O', quoth the Salmon, 'sister, be at peace:
Thank Jupiter, we both have pass'd the Net,
Our value never can be truly known,   135
Till in the Fisher's basket we be shown;
I'th' Market then my price may be the higher,
Even when I am nearest to the Cook, and fire.'
So, to great men, the moral may be stretched.
Men oft are valued high, when th'are most wretch'd.   140
But come: whither you please. I am arm'd 'gainst misery:
Bent to all sways of the oppressor's will.
There's no deep valley, but near some great hill.   *Ex[eunt].*

Act IV, Scene i

[*Enter* FERDINAND *and* BOSOLA]

FERDINAND
How doth our sister Duchess bear herself
In her imprisonment?
BOSOLA   Nobly: I'll describe her:
She's sad, as one long us'd to't: and she seems
Rather to welcome the end of misery
Than shun it: a behaviour so noble,   5
As gives a majesty to adversity:
You may discern the shape of loveliness
More perfect in her tears, than in her smiles;
She will muse four hours together: and her silence,
Methinks, expresseth more than if she spake.   10
FERDINAND
Her melancholy seems to be fortifi'd
With a strange disdain.
BOSOLA   'Tis so: and this restraint
(Like English mastives, that grow fierce with tying)

---

143 i.e. in deep depression one finds a source of strength nearby. Cf. Psalm 121.
Act IV, Scenes i and ii Lucas suggests that, for the original audience, a location
'Somewhere in Prison' was sufficient. In view of the conflicting evidence within
the play – cf. III.v.104; IV.i.1–2; IV.ii.367; V.ii.121; V.iii.s.d and 1–2 – one cannot
and need not be more precise. See Lucas II, 177 and M.C. Bradbrook, *Themes
and Conventions of Elizabethan Tragedy* (2nd edn, 1980), pp. 15, 190.

3 *long us'd* Q1 (us'd Qq2–4)

Makes her too passionately apprehend
Those pleasures she's kept from.
FERDINAND   Curse upon her!   15
I will no longer study in the book
Of another's heart: inform her what I told you.   *Exit.*

[BOSOLA *draws the traverse to reveal the* DUCHESS, CARIOLA *and*
SERVANTS]

BOSOLA
All comfort to your Grace; –
DUCHESS   I will have none.
'Pray-thee, why dost thou wrap thy poison'd pills
In gold and sugar?   20
BOSOLA
Your elder brother the Lord Ferdinand
Is come to visit you: and sends you word
'Cause once he rashly made a solemn vow
Never to see you more; he comes i'th' night;
And prays you, gently, neither torch nor taper   25
Shine in your chamber: he will kiss your hand;
And reconcile himself: but, for his vow,
He dares not see you.
DUCHESS   At his pleasure.
Take hence the lights: he's come.

[*Exeunt* SERVANTS *with lights*]

[*Enter* FERDINAND]

FERDINAND   Where are you?
DUCHESS   Here sir.
FERDINAND
This darkness suits you well.
DUCHESS   I would ask your pardon.   30
FERDINAND
You have it;
For I account it the honorabl'st revenge
Where I may kill, to pardon: where are your cubs?

19 *'Pray-thee* Qq1–2 (Pray-thee Q3; Prithee Q4)
19–20 Cf. *2 Henry VI*, III.ii.45:
         Hide not thy poison with such sugre'd words . . .
     and *The White Devil* III.ii.188–89:
         VITTORIA   I discern poison
              Under your gilded pills.
     ' "Gild" is the ordinary medical term, not a metaphor' (Dent, p. 111).
21 *elder brother* historically accurate; in the play this is only Bosola's impression.
     Cf. IV.ii.261–63.

DUCHESS
  Whom?
FERDINAND
  Call them your children;   35
  For though our national law distinguish bastards
  From true legitimate issue, compassionate nature
  Makes them all equal.
DUCHESS   Do you visit me for this?
  You violate a sacrament o'th' Church
  Shall make you howl in hell for't.
FERDINAND   It had been well,   40
  Could you have liv'd thus always: for indeed
  You were too much i'th' light. But no more;
  I come to seal my peace with you: here's a hand,
                           Gives her a dead man's hand.
  To which you have vow'd much love: the ring upon't
  You gave.
DUCHESS   I affectionately kiss it.   45
FERDINAND
  Pray do: and bury the print of it in your heart.
  I will leave this ring with you, for a love-token:
  And the hand, as sure as the ring: and do not doubt
  But you shall have the heart too. When you need a friend
  Send it to him that ow'd it: you shall see   50
  Whether he can aid you.
DUCHESS   You are very cold.
  I fear you are not well after your travel:
  Ha! Lights: Oh horrible!
FERDINAND   Let her have lights enough.   [*Exit*]

[*Enter* SERVANTS *with lights*]

39 *sacrament o' th' Church* M.C. Bradbrook comments that the Duchess 'had
   not sought the sacrament of marriage in the Church, or that of baptism,
   but she is at present experiencing the sacrament of penance' (*Themes and
   Conventions*, 2nd edn, p. 198). Gunnar Boklund feels that it is to her
   marriage that the Duchess refers here (*Sources, Themes, Characters*, p. 118).
42 *i'th' light* in the public gaze
43 s.d. placed in the margin, opposite lines 43–45b. A dead man's hand was a
   powerful charm used in the cure of madness. See M.C. Bradbrook, 'Two
   Notes upon Webster', *MLR* 42 (1947), 283–84.
44 *the ring* i.e. her wedding ring, torn off by the Cardinal
50 *ow'd* owned

DUCHESS

What witchcraft doth he practise, that he hath left
A dead man's hand here? –   55

Here is discover'd, behind a traverse, the artificial figures of
ANTONIO *and his child; appearing as if they were dead.*

BOSOLA

Look you: here's the piece from which 'twas tane;
He doth present you this sad spectacle,
That now you know directly they are dead,
Hereafter you may, wisely, cease to grieve
For that which cannot be recovered.   60

DUCHESS

There is not between heaven and earth one wish
I stay for after this: it wastes me more,
Than were't my picture, fashion'd out of wax,
Stuck with a magical needle, and then buried
In some foul dunghill: and yond's an excellent property   65
For a tyrant, which I would account mercy, –

BOSOLA

What's that?

DUCHESS

If they would bind me to that lifeless trunk,

---

55 s.d. *traverse* curtain on runners

child conj. Lucas (*children* Qq) If *children* is correct, one must assume both
that Ferdinand wants the Duchess to believe that he has murdered Antonio's
elder son as well as the imprisoned children and that her instructions about
the latter before her death (IV. ii. 200-02) proceed from an extreme lapse
of memory. Clifford Leech feels that such a lapse gave an edge to the
poignancy of her maternal concern; M.C. Bradbrook that the Duchess's
'conviction that all the children are dead is behind the heavy despair of IV,
ii: it justifies the complete hopelessness of that scene as compared with IV,
i.' D.M. Bergeron, relating the wax figures to funeral and tomb effigies,
suggests that they are intended to be prophetic. See *The Duchess of Malfi*,
edited by F. L. Lucas (1958) p. 214; Clifford Leech, *Webster: The Duchess
of Malfi*, p. 22; M. C. Bradbrook, *Themes and Conventions* 2nd edn, p. 203;
D. M. Bergeron, 'The Wax Figures in *The Duchess of Malfi*', *SEL* 18 (1978),
331–39. In Stratford in 1989 the RSC actors representing Antonio and the
children – not effigies – hung over the upper stage railing. See The Actors'
Names, 16n (p. 2); III. i. 6–8n.

58 *directly* straightforwardly

61 *earth* Q1, Q4 (the earth Qq2–3)

65–66 See D. M. Bergeron, 'Webster's Allusion to the *Second Maiden's Tragedy*',
ELN 17 (1980), 253–55, for an account of the way the Tyrant corresponds
to the figure unexpectedly and pointedly alluded to by the Duchess.

And let me freeze to death.

BOSOLA   Come, you must live.

DUCHESS

That's the greatest torture souls feel in hell,   70
In hell: that they must live, and cannot die.
Portia, I'll new kindle thy coals again,
And revive the rare and almost dead example
Of a loving wife.

BOSOLA   O fie! despair? remember
You are a Christian.

DUCHESS   The Church enjoins fasting: 75
I'll starve myself to death.

BOSOLA   Leave this vain sorrow;
Things being at the worst, begin to mend:
The bee when he hath shot his sting into your hand
May then play with your eyelid.

DUCHESS   Good comfortable fellow
Persuade a wretch that's broke upon the wheel   80
To have all his bones new set: entreat him live,
To be executed again. Who must dispatch me?
I account this world a tedious theatre,
For I do play a part in't 'gainst my will.

BOSOLA

Come, be of comfort, I will save your life.   85

DUCHESS

Indeed I have not leisure to tend so small a business.

BOSOLA

Now, by my life, I pity you.

DUCHESS   Thou art a fool then,
To waste thy pity on a thing so wretch'd
As cannot pity itself. I am full of daggers.
Puff! let me blow these vapours from me.   90

[*Enter* SERVANT]

What are you?

SERVANT   One that wishes you long life.

DUCHESS

I would thou wert hang'd for the horrible curse
Thou hast given me: I shall shortly grow one

---

72 *Portia*, Brutus' wife, choked herself by keeping hot coals in her mouth after
   hearing of her husband's defeat and suicide at Philippi.

89 *itself* Q4 (it Qq1–3)

90 *vapours* ed. (vipers Qq) The arguments advanced by Brown in support of
   his conjecture seem to me to warrant its substitution for the Qq reading:
   see Brown, p. 113.

    Of the miracles of pity. I'll go pray. No,
    I'll go curse.
BOSOLA   Oh fie!
DUCHESS   I could curse the stars.
BOSOLA   Oh fearful!   95
DUCHESS
    And those three smiling seasons of the year
    Into a Russian winter: nay the world
    To its first chaos.
BOSOLA
    Look you, the stars shine still.
DUCHESS   Oh, but you must
    Remember, my curse hath a great way to go: 100
    Plagues, that make lanes through largest families,
    Consume them.
BOSOLA   Fie lady!
DUCHESS   Let them like tyrants
    Never be rememb'red, but for the ill they have done:
    Let all the zealous prayers of mortified
    Churchmen forget them, –
BOSOLA   O uncharitable!   105
DUCHESS
    Let Heaven, a little while, cease crowning martyrs
    To punish them.
    Go, howl them this: and say I long to bleed.
    It is some mercy when men kill with speed. Exit [*with* SERVANTS].

             [*Enter* FERDINAND]

FERDINAND
    Excellent; as I would wish: she's plagu'd in art.   110
    These presentations are but fram'd in wax
    By the curious master in that quality,
    Vincentio Lauriola, and she takes them
    For true substantial bodies.
BOSOLA   Why do you do this?
FERDINAND
    To bring her to despair.
BOSOLA   'Faith, end here;   115

---

113 *Vincentio Lauriola* has not been identified.
115 *'Faith* i'faith, a common interjection in Webster's day

       And go no farther in your cruelty,
       Send her a penitential garment, to put on
       Next to her delicate skin, and furnish her
       With beads and prayerbooks.

FERDINAND   Damn her! that body of hers,
       While that my blood ran pure in't, was more worth   120
       Than that which thou wouldst comfort, call'd a soul.
       I will send her masques of common courtesans,
       Have her meat serv'd up by bawds and ruffians,
       And, 'cause she'll needs be mad, I am resolv'd
       To remove forth the common hospital   125
       All the mad folk, and place them near her lodging:
       There let them practise together, sing, and dance,
       And act their gambols to the full o'th' moon:
       If she can sleep the better for it, let her.
       Your work is almost ended.

BOSOLA   Must I see her again?   130

FERDINAND
       Yes.

BOSOLA   Never.

FERDINAND   You must.

BOSOLA   Never in mine own shape;
       That's forfeited by my intelligence,
       And this last cruel lie: when you send me next,
       The business shall be comfort.

FERDINAND   Very likely:
       Thy pity is nothing of kin to thee. Antonio   135
       Lurks about Milan; thou shalt shortly thither,
       To feed a fire as great as my revenge,
       Which nev'r will slack, till it have spent his fuel;
       Intemperate agues make physicians cruel.   *Exeunt.*

---

117 *a penitential garment* Bosola implies that the Duchess should be punished
    as an adulteress, the sentence for whom, passed by the ecclesiastical courts,
    was that they should walk through the streets in a penitential garment of
    white, carrying a lighted taper. So Jane Shore in Heywood's *Second Part of
    King Edward the Fourth* (1599) appears barefoot, in a white sheet, with her
    hair about her ears and a wax taper in her hand, and Jessica exclaims, 'What,
    must I hold a candle to my shames?' (*The Merchant of Venice* II.vi.41).

125 *remove forth* remove forth from
132 *my intelligence* my acting as an intelligencer
133 *cruel lie* Qq1–2 (cruelty Qq3–4)

Scene ii

[Enter DUCHESS *and* CARIOLA]

DUCHESS

What hideous noise was that?

CARIOLA   'Tis the wild consort

Of madmen, lady, which your tyrant brother

Hath plac'd about your lodging. This tyranny,

I think, was never practis'd till this hour.

DUCHESS

Indeed I thank him: nothing but noise, and folly   5

Can keep me in my right wits, whereas reason

And silence make me stark mad. Sit down,

Discourse to me some dismal tragedy.

CARIOLA

O 'twill increase your melancholy.

DUCHESS   Thou art deceiv'd;

To hear of greater grief would lessen mine.   10

This is a prison?

CARIOLA   Yes, but you shall live

To shake this durance off.

DUCHESS   Thou art a fool:

The robin red-breast and the nightingale

Never live long in cages.

CARIOLA   Pray dry your eyes.

What think you of Madam?   15

DUCHESS

Of nothing:

When I muse thus, I sleep.

CARIOLA

Like a madman, with your eyes open?

DUCHESS

Dost thou think we shall know one another

In th'other world?

CARIOLA   Yes, out of question.   20

Act IV, Scene ii Lucas commented that 'to the audiences of the Globe, madness was primarily funny ... Even the marriage-festival of the Princess Elizabeth was cheered with a masque of lunatics.' Notable critical appreciations of this scene are found in: Charles Lamb, *Specimens of English Dramatic Poets, who lived About the Time of Shakespeare* (1808), p. 217; S.I. Hayakawa, 'A Note on the madmen's scene in Webster's *The Duchess of Malfi*', *PMLA* 47 (1932), 907–9; C.W. Davies, 'The Structure of *The Duchess of Malfi*: An Approach', *English* 12 (1958), 89–93; Inga-Stina Ekeblad, 'The Impure Art of John Webster', *RES* n.s. 9 (1958), 253–67 (but see Boklund, *Sources, Themes, Characters*, pp. 111–12; 182 n.2).

1 *consort* collection of musicians who sing and play together

DUCHESS

  O that it were possible we might
  But hold some two days' conference with the dead,
  From them I should learn somewhat, I am sure
  I never shall know here. I'll tell thee a miracle,
  I am not mad yet, to my cause of sorrow.   25
  Th'heaven o'er my head seems made of molten brass,
  The earth of flaming sulphur, yet I am not mad.
  I am acquainted with sad misery,
  As the tann'd galley-slave is with his oar.
  Necessity makes me suffer constantly.   30
  And custom makes it easy. Who do I look like now?

CARIOLA

  Like to your picture in the gallery,
  A deal of life in show, but none in practice:
  Or rather like some reverend monument
  Whose ruins are even pitied.

DUCHESS   Very proper: 35
  And Fortune seems only to have her eyesight,
  To behold my tragedy.
  How now! what noise is that?

[Enter SERVANT]

SERVANT   I am come to tell you,
  Your brother hath intended you some sport.
  A great physician when the Pope was sick   40
  Of a deep melancholy, presented him
  With several sorts of madmen, which wild object,
  Being full of change and sport, forc'd him to laugh,
  And so th'imposthume broke: the selfsame cure
  The Duke intends on you.

DUCHESS   Let them come in.   45

24–25 In 'Further borrowings in Webster and Marston', *N&Q* n.s. 19 (1972),
    452–53, G.K. Hunter identifies Webster's source in Marston's *Antonio's*
    Revenge II.ii.144–46:
    ANTONIO ... I'll tell you wondrous strange, strange news.
    MARIA What, my good boy, stark mad?
    ANTONIO I am not. (p. 452)
26–27 Cf. Deuteronomy 28.15–34 and see Bradbrook, 'Two Notes upon Web-
    ster', p. 281.
44 *imposthume* abscess
45 *them* Q1 ('em Q4; me Qq2–3)

SERVANT

There's a mad lawyer, and a secular priest,
A doctor that hath forfeited his wits
By jealousy; an astrologian,
That in his works said such a day o'th' month
Should be the day of doom; and, failing of't,   50
Ran mad; an English tailor, craz'd i'th' brain
With the study of new fashion; a gentleman usher
Quite beside himself with care to keep in mind
The number of his lady's salutations,
Or 'How do you?' she employ'd him in each morning: 55
A farmer too, an excellent knave in grain,
Mad, 'cause he was hind'red transportation;
And let one broker, that's mad, loose to these,
You'ld think the devil were among them.

DUCHESS

Sit Cariola: let them loose when you please,   60
For I am chain'd to endure all your tyranny.

[*Enter* MADMEN]

Here, by a madman, this song is sung to a dismal kind of music.

O let us howl, some heavy note,
*   some deadly-dogged howl,*
Sounding, as from the threat'ning throat,
*   of beasts, and fatal fowl.*   65
As ravens, screech-owls, bulls, and bears,
*   We'll bell, and bawl our parts,*
Till yerksome noise, have cloy'd your ears,
*   and corrosiv'd your hearts.*

46 *secular priest* one not belonging to a monastic order
52 *fashion* Q1 (fashions Qq2–4)
56 *knave in grain* (1) a knave in the grain trade; (2) an ingrained knave
57 *transportation* export. For the topical significance of this allusion see Lucas II, p. 182.
58 *broker* dealer in goods or flesh (i.e. a procurer)
60–61 a reference to the chaining-up of mad people. Cf. I.ii.337–38.
61 s.d. *a madman* possibly the mad broker. Frank B. Fieler, in 'The Eight Madmen in *The Duchess of Malfi*', *SEL* 7 (1967), 343–50, assigns the speeches of ll. 74–113 to seven of the madmen described by the servant and this song to the broker, for whom no speech is appropriate, but who seems well qualified to sing these words.
62–73 The music for this typical mad song survives in three seventeenth-century MSS, and is reproduced in Brown's edition.
67 *bell* Qq2–4 bellow (bill Q1)
68 *yerksome* irksome
69 *corrosiv'd* Q4 corroded (corasiv'd Qq1–3)

> *At last when as our quire wants breath,*   70
>   *our bodies being blest,*
> *We'll sing like swans, to welcome death,*
>   *and die in love and rest.*

[MAD ASTROLOGER]   Doomsday not come yet? I'll draw it
nearer by a perspective, or make a glass, that shall set all the   75
world on fire upon an instant. I cannot sleep, my pillow is
stuff'd with a litter of porcupines.

[MAD LAWYER]   Hell is a mere glass-house, where the devils
are continually blowing up women's souls on hollow irons,
and the fire never goes out.   80

[MAD PRIEST]   I will lie with every woman in my parish
the tenth night: I will tithe them over like haycocks.

[MAD DOCTOR]   Shall my pothecary outgo me, because I am
a cuckold? I have found out his roguery: he makes allum of
his wife's urine, and sells it to Puritans, that have sore   85
throats with over-straining.

[MAD USHER]   I have skill in heraldry.

[MAD TAILOR]   Hast?

[MAD USHER]   You do give for your crest a woodcock's
head, with the brains pick'd out on't. You are a very ancient   90
gentleman.

[MAD PRIEST]   Greek is turn'd Turk; we are only to be sav'd
by the Helvetian translation.

74ff. Eight madmen are described by the servant (ll. 46–59) and the same
number dance (113 s.d.), but Qq1–3 assign speeches to four only, identified
by number. Q4 identifies them as Astrologer, Taylor, Priest and Doctor
respectively; Lucas as [Astrologer], [Lawyer], [Priest] and [Doctor]. Brown
noted (p. 120) that only the fourth – the doctor – was consistently characterized. Considering their grouping on stage as well as the content of their
speeches, Frank B. Fieler ('The Eight Madmen') proposed the identi-
fications which I have adopted here. In performance, the number of speaking
parts may vary according to the number of actors and types of costume
available. See also Additional Notes, p. 136.

75 *perspective* telescope; magnifying glass

78 *glass-house* glass factory

79 *women's* Q1 (men's Qq2–4)

89 The woodcock was considered to be brainless.

92–93 A satirical embodiment of a Jacobean Puritan parson (as he is described
in Q4 actors' list), not an early sixteenth-century Italian secular priest, the
mad priest here expresses disapproval of all English versions of the Bible
save *the Helvetian translation*: i.e. the Calvinistic Geneva Bible of 1560. By
Greek is turn'd Turk he means that, in the 1609–10 Douay and 1611 King
James versions, the Greek New Testament has become Moslem or infidel,
by being put to the service of the wrong faith.

[MAD LAWYER]   Come on sir, I will lay the law to
    you.   95
[MAD FARMER]   Oh, rather lay a corrosive, the law will eat
    to the bone.
[MAD PRIEST]   He that drinks but to satisfy nature is damn'd.
[MAD ASTROLOGER]   If I had my glass here, I would show a sight
    should make all the women here call me mad doctor.   100
[MAD TAILOR, *pointing to* MAD PRIEST] What's he, a rope-
maker?
[MAD USHER]   No, no, no, a snuffling knave, that while he
    shows the tombs, will have his hand in a wench's placket.
[MAD DOCTOR]   Woe to the caroche that brought home my   105
    wife from the masque, at three o'clock in the morning; it
    had a large feather bed in it.
[MAD FARMER]   I have pared the devil's nails forty times,
    roasted them in raven's eggs, and cur'd agues with them.
[MAD ASTROLOGER]   Get me three hundred milch bats, to make   110
    possets to procure sleep.
[MAD DOCTOR]   All the college may throw their caps at me, I
    have made a soap-boiler costive: it was my masterpiece:–

> *Here the dance consisting of 8. madmen, with music answerable*
> *thereunto, after which* BOSOLA, *like an old man, enters.*

DUCHESS
    Is he mad too?
SERVANT   Pray question him; I'll leave you.
                                    [*Exeunt* SERVANT *and* MADMEN]
BOSOLA
    I am come to make thy tomb.
DUCHESS   Ha! my tomb?   115
    Thou speak'st as if I lay upon my death-bed,
    Gasping for breath: dost thou perceive me sick?

94–95 *lay the law* expound the law
96 *lay a corrosive* apply a corrosive
101–2 *ropemaker* i.e. in league with the hangman
104 *placket* opening in a skirt
111 *possets* hot milk curdled by spiced wine or ale
112 *throw their caps at* may do their utmost against me but it will be in vain
    (Lucas)
113 *costive* constipated. Soap being used in suppositories to loosen the bowels,
    diarrhoea was an occupational hazard for soap-boilers.
113 s.d. *old man* Qq1–3 (*Old Bell-Man* Q4); see IV.ii.170–71n. Forker suggests
    that the aged figure, 'as in Chaucer's *Pardoner's Tale*, symbolizes human
    mortality, if he does not quite personify death' (p. 339).

BOSOLA   Yes, and the more dangerously, since thy sickness
   is insensible.
DUCHESS   Thou art not mad, sure; dost know me?   120
BOSOLA   Yes.
DUCHESS   Who am I?
BOSOLA   Thou art a box of worm seed, at best, but a salvatory of green mummy: what's this flesh? a little cruded
   milk, fantastical puff-paste: our bodies are weaker than those   125
   paper prisons boys use to keep flies in: more contemptible;
   since ours is to preserve earth-worms: didst thou ever see
   a lark in a cage? such is the soul in the body: this world
   is like her little turf of grass, and the heaven o'er our heads,
   like her looking-glass, only gives us a miserable knowledge   130
   of the small compass of our prison.
DUCHESS   Am not I thy Duchess?
BOSOLA   Thou art some great woman, sure; for riot begins
   to sit on thy forehead (clad in grey hairs) twenty years sooner
   than on a merry milkmaid's. Thou sleep'st worse, than if a   135
   mouse should be forc'd to take up her lodging in a cat's ear:
   a little infant, that breeds its teeth, should it lie with thee,
   would cry out, as if thou wert the more unquiet bedfellow.
DUCHESS   I am Duchess of Malfi still.
BOSOLA   That makes thy sleeps so broken: 140
   Glories, like glow-worms, afar off shine bright,
   But look'd to near, have neither heat nor light.
DUCHESS   Thou art very plain.
BOSOLA   My trade is to flatter the dead, not the living;
   I am a tomb-maker.   145
DUCHESS   And thou com'st to make my tomb?
BOSOLA   Yes.

---

119 *insensible* imperceptible
123 The punctuation of Q1 is equivocal, and may be modernized as: (1) Thou
   art a box of worm-seed; at best but a . . .; (2) Thou art a box of worm-seed,
   at best; but a . . .
123–24 *salvatory* ointment box
124 *green* As Brown suggests (p. 123), this is 'presumably a quibble to suggest
   a "living" corpse, or flesh that is not "ripe" enough to be mummy'.
   mummy mummia, a medicinal preparation made from Egyptian mummies
   cruded Q1 curdled (curded Qq2–4)
125 *puff-paste* a particularly light pastry, containing a lot of air
127 *ever* Q1 (never Qq2–4)
133–38 These lines provide a bitter commentary on III.ii.11–13, 58–60.
136 *her* Q1 (his Qq2–4)
140 *sleeps* Qq1–2 (sleep Qq3–4)
141–42 The lines are repeated verbatim from *The White Devil* V.i.40–41.
142 *to* Q1, Q3 (too Q2; on Q4)

DUCHESS

    Let me be a little merry;
    Of what stuff wilt thou make it?

BOSOLA

    Nay, resolve me first, of what fashion?   150

DUCHESS

    Why, do we grow fantastical in our death-bed?
    Do we affect fashion in the grave?

BOSOLA

    Most ambitiously. Princes' images on their tombs
    Do not lie as they were wont, seeming to pray
    Up to Heaven: but with their hands under their cheeks,   155
    As if they died of the tooth-ache; they are not carved
    With their eyes fix'd upon the stars; but as
    Their minds were wholly bent upon the world,
    The self-same way they seem to turn their faces.

DUCHESS

    Let me know fully therefore the effect   160
    Of this thy dismal preparation,
    This talk, fit for a charnel.

BOSOLA   Now I shall;

        [*Enter* EXECUTIONERS *with*] *a coffin, cords, and a bell.*

    Here is a present from your princely brothers,
    And may it arrive welcome, for it brings
    Last benefit, last sorrow.

DUCHESS   Let me see it.   165
    I have so much obedience, in my blood,
    I wish it in their veins, to do them good.

BOSOLA

    This is your last presence chamber.

150 *resolve* explain
153–59 The allusion here is to a change in English tomb sculpture from the late
    medieval portrayal of the deceased as a recumbent figure to a more relaxed
    treatment of the effigy which included a reclining attitude with the figure
    'propped up' on one elbow. Effigies whose hands are *under their cheeks* / *As
    if they died of the tooth-ache* include those of Thomas Owen (d. 1598) in
    Westminster Abbey and Lady Mary Eure (d. 1613) in Ludlow, Salop. See
    Brian Kemp, *English Church Monuments* (London, 1980), pp. 78–80. In St
    Ethelreda's Church, Hatfield, Herts., a single monument represents Dame
    Agnes Saunders (d. 1588) propped up on one elbow, with her hand on a
    skull, and her daughter Dame Elizabeth Moore (d. 1612) lying above and
    slightly behind her, with her head resting on her cheek. Dame Agnes, who
    had been twice widowed, died giving birth to Elizabeth, the daughter of her
    third husband. See also Additional Notes, p. 135.
162 *charnel* Q1, Q4 (chamell Q2; chamel Q3)

CARIOLA

O my sweet lady!

DUCHESS   Peace; it affrights not me.

BOSOLA

I am the common bellman,   170

That usually is sent to condemn'd persons,

The night before they suffer.

DUCHESS   Even now thou said'st

Thou wast a tomb-maker?

BOSOLA   'Twas to bring you

By degrees to mortification. Listen: [*Rings the bell*]

Hark, now every thing is still,   175

The screech-owl and the whistler shrill

Call upon our Dame, aloud,

And bid her quickly don her shroud.

Much you had of land and rent,

Your length in clay's now competent.   180

A long war disturb'd your mind,

Here your perfect peace is sign'd.

Of what is't fools make such vain keeping?

Sin their conception, their birth, weeping:

Their life, a general mist of error,   185

Their death, a hideous storm of terror.

170–71 In 1605 Robert Dowe (or Dove) of the Merchant Taylors' Company gave an endowment of £50 to the clerk of St Sepulcre's to toll a handbell outside the cells of condemned prisoners in Newgate at midnight before their executions and recite lines of exhortation to repentance. As a fellow member of the Merchant Taylors' Company, John Webster's father was one of the signatories of the endowment. Dowe having died in 1612, the performance of this office would have been known to Webster's audience to whom it would thus be clear that the Duchess had been condemned to death. Cf. IV.ii.294–98. The bell and a description of this and other ceremonies prescribed by Dowe may be viewed in St Sepulcre's. Cf. Forker, pp. 21–24.

174 *mortification* (1) freedom from earthly concerns; (2) state of insensibility or torpor before death

176 *whistler* a bird such as the ring ouzel, widgeon or lapwing, the whistling cry of which was considered an ill omen

179 *rent* revenue, income

180 *competent* of sufficient means for comfortable living

182 *peace* treaty; in the form 'Quietus' this would remind the Duchess of her own use of that term. See I.ii.377–80; III.ii.187 and cf. *Hamlet* III.i.75–76.

183 *keeping* taking care of; retaining

186 *terror* Q1, Q4 (error Qq2–3)

Strew your hair with powders sweet:
Don clean linen, bath your feet,
And, the foul fiend more to check,
A crucifix let bless your neck.   190
'Tis now full tide 'tween night and day,
End your groan, and come away.

[EXECUTIONERS *approach*]

CARIOLA
Hence villains, tyrants, murderers. Alas!
What will you do with my lady? Call for help.
DUCHESS
To whom, to our next neighbours? They are mad-folks.   195
BOSOLA
Remove that noise.

[EXECUTIONERS *seize* CARIOLA, *who struggles*]

DUCHESS   Farewell Cariola,
In my last will I have not much to give;
A many hungry guests have fed upon me,
Thine will be a poor reversion.
CARIOLA   I will die with her.
DUCHESS
I pray thee look thou giv'st my little boy   200
Some syrup for his cold, and let the girl
Say her prayers, ere she sleep.   [CARIOLA *is forced off*]
                              Now what you please,
What death?
BOSOLA   Strangling: here are your executioners.
DUCHESS
I forgive them:

187–90 The Duchess is told to prepare her own body for burial, with the
    implication that there will be none to do that office after her death. The
    reference to the crucifix suggests that there will be no religious ceremony,
    either.
188 *bath* Q1, Q4 (bathe Qq2–3)
190 *bless* make the sign of the cross on
199 *reversion* something inherited upon the death of the holder
200–02 See IV.i.55 s.d. note. The Duchess's commands remind us of Antonio's
    injunction at III.v.81–83. Inga-Stina Ewbank comments that Webster's
    genuine evocation of 'normal, domestic, love' in the relationship between
    Antonio and the Duchess makes these lines 'part of a *felt* context and not
    just an incidental piece of sentimentality': 'A Cunning Piece Wrought
    Perspective' in *John Webster*, edited by Brian Morris, Mermaid Critical
    Commentaries, pp. 157–78 (p. 172).

The apoplexy, catarrh, or cough o'th' lungs   205
Would do as much as they do.

BOSOLA

Doth not death fright you?   Who would be afraid on't?

DUCHESS

Knowing to meet such excellent company
In th'other world.

BOSOLA   Yet, methinks,
The manner of your death should much afflict you,   210
This cord should terrify you?

DUCHESS   Not a whit:
What would it pleasure me, to have my throat cut
With diamonds? or to be smothered
With cassia? or to be shot to death, with pearls?
I know death hath ten thousand several doors   215
For men to take their *Exits*: and 'tis found
They go on such strange geometrical hinges,
You may open them both ways: any way, for Heaven sake,
So I were out of your whispering. Tell my brothers
That I perceive death, now I am well awake,   220
Best gift is, they can give, or I can take.
I would fain put off my last woman's fault,
I'll'd not be tedious to you.

EXECUTIONERS   We are ready.

DUCHESS

Dispose my breath how please you, but my body
Bestow upon my women, will you?

EXECUTIONERS   Yes.   225

DUCHESS

Pull, and pull strongly, for your able strength
Must pull down heaven upon me:
Yet stay, heaven gates are not so highly arch'd
As princes' palaces: they that enter there
Must go upon their knees. [*Kneels*] Come violent death,   230

---

205 *catarrh* cerebral effusion or haemorrhage
215–18 The basis of this striking image is the Virgilian 'Mille viae mortis', also
a Senecan commonplace. Webster could have found it in Montaigne, Florio,
Marston or the plays of Fletcher. The reference to the geometrical hinges
which enable men to open the doors both ways is best interpreted as
indicating an antithesis between committing suicide and being murdered.
See R.F. Whitman, 'Webster's "Duchess of Malfi" ', *N&Q* n.s. 6 (1959),
174; Bradbrook, *Themes and Conventions*, 2nd edn, pp. 82–84.
218 See III.v.79–80n.
229 *princes'* Q1 (princely Qq2–4)

Serve for mandragora to make me sleep;
Go tell my brothers, when I am laid out,
They then may feed in quiet.   *They strangle her.*
BOSOLA   Where's the waiting woman?
Fetch her. Some other strangle the children.
               [*Exeunt* EXECUTIONERS. *Enter one with* CARIOLA]
Look you, there sleeps your mistress.   235
CARIOLA   O you are damn'd
Perpetually for this. My turn is next,
Is't not so ordered?
BOSOLA   Yes, and I am glad
You are so well prepar'd for't.
CARIOLA   You are deceiv'd sir,
I am not prepar'd for't. I will not die,
I will first come to my answer; and know   240
How I have offended.
BOSOLA   Come, dispatch her.
You kept her counsel, now you shall keep ours.
CARIOLA
I will not die, I must not, I am contracted
To a young gentleman.
EXECUTIONER [*Showing the noose*] Here's your wedding-ring.
CARIOLA
Let me but speak with the Duke. I'll discover   245
Treason to his person.
BOSOLA   Delays: throttle her.
EXECUTIONER
She bites: and scratches.
CARIOLA   If you kill me now
I am damn'd. I have not been at confession
This two years.
BOSOLA   When!
CARIOLA   I am quick with child.
BOSOLA   Why then,
Your credit's sav'd: bear her into th' next room.   250
Let this lie still.

          [EXECUTIONERS *strangle* CARIOLA *and exeunt with her body.*
                    Enter FERDINAND]

FERDINAND   Is she dead?
BOSOLA   She is what

---

231 *mandragora* mandrake plant, taken by Webster's contemporaries to be a
     kind of narcotic   235 *you are* Q1 (thou art Qq2–4)
237 *and I* Q1 (I Qq2–4)   240 *will first* Q1 (will Qq2–4)
249 *When!* See II.i.117n.   250 *th'* Qq1–2 (the Qq3–4)

You'll'd have her. But here begin your pity,

[BOSOLA *draws the traverse and*] *Shows the children strangled.*

Alas, how have these offended?
FERDINAND   The death
Of young wolves is never to be pitied.
BOSOLA
Fix your eye here.
FERDINAND   Constantly.
BOSOLA   Do you not weep?   255
Other sins only speak; murther shrieks out:
The element of water moistens the earth,
But blood flies upwards, and bedews the heavens.
FERDINAND
Cover her face. Mine eyes dazzle: she di'd young.
BOSOLA
I think not so: her infelicity   260
Seem'd to have years too many.
FERDINAND   She and I were twins:
And should I die this instant, I had liv'd
Her time to a minute.
BOSOLA   It seems she was born first:
You have bloodily approv'd the ancient truth,
That kindred commonly do worse agree   265
Than remote strangers.
FERDINAND   Let me see her face again;
Why didst not thou pity her? What an excellent
Honest man might'st thou have been
If thou hadst borne her to some sanctuary!
Or, bold in a good cause, oppos'd thyself   270
With thy advanced sword above thy head,
Between her innocence and my revenge!
I bad thee, when I was distracted of my wits,
Go kill my dearest friend, and thou hast done't.

264 *approv'd* confirmed, demonstrated
265 *agree* Qq2–4 (ageee Q1)
269 *some sanctuary* some place, such as a church, where, according to medieval ecclesiastical law, a fugitive from justice was entitled to freedom from arrest
272 *innocence* Q1, Q4 (innocency Qq2–3)
274 *friend* 'In Renaissance usage the term "friend" sometimes meant lover or paramour' (Forker, p. 308); cf. *Measure for Measure* I.iv.29: 'He hath got his friend with child.'
done't ed. (don't Qq)

For let me but examine well the cause;   275
What was the meanness of her match to me?
Only I must confess, I had a hope,
Had she continu'd widow, to have gain'd
An infinite mass of treasure by her death:
And that was the main cause; her marriage,   280
That drew a stream of gall quite through my heart;
For thee, (as we observe in tragedies
That a good actor many times is curs'd
For playing a villain's part) I hate thee for't:
And, for my sake, say thou hast done much ill, well.   285

BOSOLA
Let me quicken your memory: for I perceive
You are falling into ingratitude. I challenge
The reward due to my service.
FERDINAND   I'll tell thee,
What I'll give thee –
BOSOLA   Do.
FERDINAND   I'll give thee a pardon
For this murther.
BOSOLA   Ha?
FERDINAND   Yes: and 'tis   290
The largest bounty I can study to do thee.
By what authority didst thou execute
This bloody sentence?
BOSOLA   By yours.
FERDINAND   Mine? Was I her judge?
Did any ceremonial form of law
Doom her to not-being? did a complete jury   295
Deliver her conviction up i'th' court?
Where shalt thou find this judgment register'd
Unless in hell? See: like a bloody fool
Th'hast forfeited thy life, and thou shalt die for't.
BOSOLA
The office of justice is perverted quite   300

---

280 *that* Q1 (what Qq2–4)
     cause; Qq1–2 (cause? Qq3–4)
282–84 Richard Burbage, the most distinguished of the King's Men and prob-
     ably the most famous Elizabethan actor, took the part of Ferdinand in early
     performances of the play. According to the Actors' list of Qq1–2, the part
     was later taken by J. Taylor, who joined the company after Burbage's death.
293 *sentence* Q1 (service Qq2–4)
297 *judgment* Qq2–4 (ludgment Q1)

When one thief hangs another: who shall dare
To reveal this?
FERDINAND   Oh, I'll tell thee:
The wolf shall find her grave, and scrape it up;
Not to devour the corpse, but to discover
The horrid murther.
BOSOLA   You; not I shall quake for't.   305
FERDINAND
Leave me.
BOSOLA   I will first receive my pension.
FERDINAND
You are a villain.
BOSOLA   When your ingratitude
Is judge, I am so –
FERDINAND   O horror!
That not the fear of him which binds the devils
Can prescribe man obedience.   310
Never look upon me more.
BOSOLA   Why fare thee well:
Your brother and yourself are worthy men;
You have a pair of hearts are hollow graves,
Rotten, and rotting others: and your vengeance,
Like two chain'd bullets, still goes arm in arm;   315
You may be brothers: for treason, like the plague,
Doth take much in a blood. I stand like one
That long hath tane a sweet and golden dream.
I am angry with myself, now that I wake.
FERDINAND
Get thee into some unknown part o'th' world   320
That I may never see thee.
BOSOLA   Let me know
Wherefore I should be thus neglected? Sir,
I served your tyranny: and rather strove
To satisfy yourself, than all the world;
And though I loath'd the evil, yet I lov'd   325
You that did counsel it: and rather sought
To appear a true servant than an honest man.
FERDINAND
I'll go hunt the badger by owl-light:
'Tis a deed of darkness.   *Exit.*

---

317 *take* ... *blood* take a strong hold in blood relatives

BOSOLA

He's much distracted. Off my painted honour!   330
While with vain hopes our faculties we tire,
We seem to sweat in ice and freeze in fire;
What would I do, were this to do again?
I would not change my peace of conscience
For all the wealth of Europe. She stirs; here's life.   335
Return, fair soul, from darkness, and lead mine
Out of this sensible hell. She's warm, she breathes:
Upon thy pale lips I will melt my heart
To store them with fresh colour. Who's there?
Some cordial drink! Alas! I dare not call: 340
So pity would destroy pity: her eye opes,
And heaven in it seems to ope, that late was shut,
To take me up to mercy.

DUCHESS   Antonio!

BOSOLA

Yes, Madam, he is living,
The dead bodies you saw were but feign'd statues;   345
He's reconcil'd to your brothers: the Pope hath wrought
The atonement.

DUCHESS   Mercy.   *She dies.*

BOSOLA

Oh, she's gone again: there the cords of life broke.

330 G.P.V. Akrigg feels that *painted honour* 'can only refer to the hypocritical pretence of love for Ferdinand made in the lines immediately preceding' ('A Phrase in Webster', *N&Q* 193 (1948), 454). McLuskie and Uglow record that in the 1980 MRE production Bosola took the phrase literally, 'removing his disfiguring face mask, implying that this speech came from the "real" Bosola' (p. 173). Bosola may refer here to the deceptive honour he has gained through his position at court, which, since it involves acting as Ferdinand's intelligencer, he now renounces. Cf. III.ii.279.

333 *were* Qq2–4 (wete Q1)

335 Cf. *Othello* V.ii.125–28 where Desdemona also revives after she has been supposed dead.

337 *sensible* perceptible, palpable

340 *cordial* heart-strengthening

341 *So pity ... pity* In calling for help, Bosola might arouse Ferdinand, who would prevent him from saving the Duchess.

341–42 *opes ... ope* Qq1–3 (opens ... open Q4)

343 *mercy* Qq2–4 (merry Q1)

347 *atonement* reconciliation
Mercy i.e. probably 'a last half-conscious appeal to her murderers to spare her' (Lucas II, 189)

348 *cords of life* nerves or sinews. Brown notes that 'heart-strings' were often spoken of as if they were tangible' (p. 135).

Oh sacred innocence, that sweetly sleeps
On turtles' feathers: whilst a guilty conscience   350
Is a black register, wherein is writ
All our good deeds and bad; a perspective
That shows us hell; that we cannot be suffer'd
To do good when we have a mind to it!
This is manly sorrow: 355
These tears, I am very certain, never grew
In my mother's milk. My estate is sunk
Below the degree of fear: where were
These penitent fountains while she was living?
Oh, they were frozen up: here is a sight   360
As direful to my soul as is the sword
Unto a wretch hath slain his father. Come,
I'll bear thee hence,
And execute thy last will; that's deliver
Thy body to the reverend dispose   365
Of some good women: that the cruel tyrant
Shall not deny me. Then I'll post to Milan,
Where somewhat I will speedily enact
Worth my dejection.   *Exit [carrying the body].*

Act V, Scene i

[*Enter* ANTONIO *and* DELIO]

ANTONIO
    What think you of my hope of reconcilement
    To the Aragonian brethren?

360–62 Such a wretch is found in *3 Henry VI*, II.v.61–72.
369 *dejection* being cast down in terms of status and spirit
Act V takes place in Milan. In 'Observation and Theatricality in Webster's *The Duchess of Malfi*', *TRI* 6 (1981), 36–44, Anat Feinberg points out that 'there is verbal evidence that every scene takes place at night' (p. 39). Its structure and content – seen in contrast to those of Act IV – have aroused considerable adverse comment. Among critics who defend it are G. Wilson Knight, who says that Act V can be seen to represent the Duchess 'buried deep in the play' ('*The Duchess of Malfi*', *MRev* 4 (1967), pp. 88–113 (p. 107)) and Charles Wilkinson, who demonstrates how 'it exhibits what happens to Ferdinand after his second self has been lost, and it repeats the doubling motif in situations where he is not directly involved . . .' ('Twin Structures in John Webster's *The Duchess of Malfi*, *L&Psy* 31 (1981), 52–65 (p. 62)). Normand Berlin's '*The Duchess of Malfi*: Act V and Genre' in *G* 3 (1970), 351–63, is another interesting contribution to the debate.

DELIO   I misdoubt it
  For though they have sent their letters of safe conduct
  For your repair to Milan, they appear
  But nets to entrap you. The Marquis of Pescara,   5
  Under whom you hold certain land in cheat,
  Much 'gainst his noble nature, hath been mov'd
  To seize those lands, and some of his dependants
  Are at this instant making it their suit
  To be invested in your revenues.   10
  I cannot think they mean well to your life,
  That do deprive you of your means of life,
  Your living.
ANTONIO   You are still an heretic.
  To any safety I can shape myself.
DELIO
  Here comes the Marquis. I will make myself   15
  Petitioner for some part of your land,
  To know whither it is flying.
ANTONIO   I pray do.

[*Enter* PESCARA]

DELIO
  Sir, I have a suit to you.
PESCARA   To me?
DELIO   An easy one:
  There is the citadel of St. Bennet,
  With some demenses, of late in the possession   20
  Of Antonio Bologna; please you bestow them on me?
PESCARA
  You are my friend. But this is such a suit
  Nor fit for me to give, nor you to take.
DELIO
  No sir?
PESCARA I will give you ample reason for't
  Soon, in private. Here's the Cardinal's mistress.   25

[*Enter* JULIA]

---

6 *in cheat* ed. (in Cheit Qq1–3; in Escheat Q4) i.e. Antonio held the land as
  tenant, but it would revert to Pescara should Antonio die without heirs or
  commit treason or other felony.
13–14 *heretic./ To* Qq1–3 (heretic/ To Q4, Dyce, Hazlitt, Vaughan, Sampson,
  Lucas, McIlwraith, Brown, Gunby)
19 *St. Bennet* St Benedict
25 *Here's* Q1, Q4 (Her's Qq2–3)

JULIA

  My lord, I am grown your poor petitioner,
  And should be an ill beggar, had I not
  A great man's letter here, the Cardinal's
  To court you in my favour.

                                   [*She gives him a letter which he reads*]

PESCARA   He entreats for you

  The citadel of Saint Bennet, that belong'd   30
  To the banish'd Bologna.

JULIA   Yes.

PESCARA

  I could not have thought of a friend I could
  Rather pleasure with it: 'tis yours.

JULIA   Sir, I thank you:

  And he shall know how doubly I am engag'd
  Both in your gift, and speediness of giving,   35
  Which makes your grant the greater.   *Exit.*

ANTONIO [*Aside*]   How they fortify

  Themselves with my ruin!

DELIO   Sir, I am

  Little bound to you.

PESCARA   Why?

DELIO

  Because you deni'd this suit to me, and gave't
  To such a creature.

PESCARA   Do you know what it was?   40

  It was Antonio's land: not forfeited
  By course of law; but ravish'd from his throat
  By the Cardinal's entreaty: it were not fit
  I should bestow so main a piece of wrong
  Upon my friend: 'tis a gratification   45
  Only due to a strumpet; for it is injustice.
  Shall I sprinkle the pure blood of innocents
  To make those followers I call my friends
  Look ruddier upon me? I am glad
  This land, tane from the owner by such wrong, 50
  Returns again unto so foul an use,
  As salary for his lust. Learn, good Delio,
  To ask noble things of me, and you shall find
  I'll be a noble giver.

DELIO   You instruct me well.

ANTONIO

  [*Aside*] Why, here's a man, now, would fright impudence 55
  From sauciest beggars.

54 *noble* Qq1–2 (nobler Qq3–4)

PESCARA   Prince Ferdinand's come to Milan
    Sick, as they give out, of an apoplexy:
    But some say 'tis a frenzy; I am going
    To visit him.   *Exit.*
ANTONIO   'Tis a noble old fellow.
DELIO
    What course do you mean to take, Antonio?   60
ANTONIO
    This night I mean to venture all my fortune,
    Which is no more than a poor ling'ring life,
    To the Cardinal's worst of malice. I have got
    Private access to his chamber: and intend
    To visit him, about the mid of night,   65
    As once his brother did our noble Duchess.
    It may be that the sudden apprehension
    Of danger (for I'll go in mine own shape)
    When he shall see it fraight with love and duty,
    May draw the poison out of him, and work   70
    A friendly reconcilement: if it fail,
    Yet it shall rid me of this infamous calling,
    For better fall once, than be ever falling.
DELIO
    I'll second you in all danger: and, howe'er,
    My life keeps rank with yours.   75
ANTONIO
    You are still my lov'd and best friend.   *Exeunt.*

Scene ii

[*Enter* PESCARA *and* DOCTOR]

PESCARA
    Now doctor, may I visit your patient?
DOCTOR
    If't please your lordship: but he's instantly
    To take the air here in the gallery,

58 *frenzy* 'an inflammation of the brain due to an invasion of choler: its
    symptoms were like those of melancholic madness, but continuous rather
    than cyclical' (Brown)
59 *old fellow* Pescara was only 36 when he died in 1525.
64 *and* Qq1–2 (and I Qq3–4)
69 *fraight* fraught

By my direction.
PESCARA   Pray thee, what's his disease?
DOCTOR
A very pestilent disease, my lord,   5
They call lycanthropia.
PESCARA   What's that?
I need a dictionary to't.
DOCTOR   I'll tell you:
In those that are possess'd with't there o'erflows
Such melancholy humour, they imagine
Themselves to be transformed into wolves.   10
Steal forth to churchyards in the dead of night,
And dig dead bodies up: as two nights since
One met the Duke, 'bout midnight in a lane
Behind St. Mark's church, with the leg of a man
Upon his shoulder; and he howl'd fearfully: 15
Said he was a wolf: only the difference
Was, a wolf's skin was hairy on the outside,
His on the inside: bad them take their swords,
Rip up his flesh, and try: straight I was sent for,
And having minister'd to him, found his Grace   20
Very well recovered.
PESCARA   I am glad on't.
DOCTOR
Yet not without some fear
Of a relapse: if he grow to his fit again
I'll go a nearer way to work with him
Than ever Paracelsus dream'd of. If   25
They'll give me leave, I'll buffet his madness out of him.
Stand aside: he comes.

        [*Enter* CARDINAL, FERDINAND, MALATESTE *and* BOSOLA, *who*
                remains in the background]

FERDINAND   Leave me.
MALATESTE   Why doth your lordship love this solitariness?

---

6 *lycanthropia* wolf-madness
8 *those* Q1, Q4 (these Qq2–3)
17 *was hairy* Q1 (is hairy Qq2–4)
20 *to* Q1 (unto Qq2–4)
24 *I'll . . . him* Q1 (Qq2–4 *omit*)
25 *Paracelsus* Q3 (Paraclesus Qq1–2; Q4 *omits*) a famous physician (1493–
   1541), who combined the studies of medicine and chemistry, and was
   reputed to be a magician, of whom many strange tales were told
29 *love* Q1 (use Qq2–4)

FERDINAND   Eagles commonly fly alone. They are crows,   30
   daws, and starlings that flock together. Look, what's that
   follows me?
MALATESTE   Nothing, my lord.
FERDINAND   Yes.
MALATESTE   'Tis your shadow.   35
FERDINAND   Stay it; let it not haunt me.
MALATESTE   Impossible, if you move, and the sun shine.
FERDINAND   I will throttle it. [*Throws himself upon his shadow*]
MALATESTE   Oh, my lord: you are angry with nothing.
FERDINAND   You are a fool. How is't possible I should   40
   catch my shadow unless I fall upon't? When I go to hell, I
   mean to carry a bribe: for look you, good gifts evermore
   make way for the worst persons.
PESCARA   Rise, good my lord.
FERDINAND   I am studying the art of patience.   45
PESCARA   'Tis a noble virtue; –
FERDINAND   To drive six snails before me, from this town
   to Moscow; neither use goad nor whip to them, but let
   them take their own time: (the patient'st man i'th' world
   match me for an experiment!) and I'll crawl after like a   50
   sheep-biter.
CARDINAL   Force him up. [*They get* FERDINAND *to his feet*]
FERDINAND
   Use me well, you were best.
   What I have done, I have done: I'll confess nothing.
DOCTOR
   Now let me come to him. Are you mad, my lord?   55
   Are you out of your princely wits?
FERDINAND   What's he?
PESCARA   Your doctor.
FERDINAND
   Let me have his beard saw'd off, and his eye-brows
   Fil'd more civil.
DOCTOR   I must do mad tricks with him,
   For that's the only way on't. I have brought

31–41 In '*The Duchess of Malfi* and Two Emblems in Whitney and Peacham',
   N&Q n.s. 29 (1982), 146–47, R.E.R. Madelaine points out that Whitney's
   Choice of Emblemes (Leyden, 1586, p. 32) depicts a man holding a sword,
   probably a murderer, who 'shows fear of his own shadow, cast by his
   standing in the moral light of Jupiter – this being an emblem of guilt' which
   the accompanying verse describes.
51 *sheep-biter* dog that worries or bites sheep
58 *Fil'd* ed. (fil'd Q1, Q4; fill'd Qq2–3)
   civil becoming

Your Grace a salamander's skin, to keep you   60
From sun-burning.
FERDINAND   I have cruel sore eyes.
DOCTOR
The white of a cocatrice's egg is present remedy.
FERDINAND
Let it be a new-laid one, you were best.
Hide me from him. Physicians are like kings,
They brook no contradiction.
DOCTOR   Now he begins   65
To fear me; now let me alone with him.

    [FERDINAND *tries to take off his gown*; CARDINAL *seizes him*]

CARDINAL
How now, put off your gown?
DOCTOR   Let me have some forty urinals filled with rose-
water: he and I'll go pelt one another with them; now he
begins to fear me. Can you fetch a frisk, sir? [*Aside to*   70
CARDINAL] Let him go, let him go upon my peril. I find by
his eye, he stands in awe of me: I'll make him as tame as a
dormouse.   [CARDINAL *releases* FERDINAND]
FERDINAND   Can you fetch your frisks, sir! I will stamp him
into a cullis; flay off his skin, to cover one of the anatomies,   75
this rogue hath set i'th' cold yonder, in Barber-Chirur-
geons' Hall. Hence, hence! you are all of you like beasts for
sacrifice, [*Throws the* DOCTOR *down and beats him*] there's
nothing left of you, but tongue and belly, flattery and
lechery.   [*Exit*]   80
PESCARA   Doctor, he did not fear you throughly.
DOCTOR   True, I was somewhat too forward.

---

62 *present* immediate
66 s.d. ed. (Qq1–3 *omit*; Q4 *puts off his four Cloaks one after another*). The comic
    business described in Q4 'is reminiscent of the many waistcoats of the
    gravedigger in *Hamlet* in the 18–19th centuries' (Brown, p. 144).
70 *fetch a frisk* cut a caper
75 *cullis* Cf. II.iv.66n.
    anatomies Qq2–4 (anotomies Q1) skeletons used in anatomical study
76–77 *Barber-Chirurgeons' Hall* contained an anatomical museum (Mc-
    Ilwraith).
78 s.d. Q4 (Qq1–3 *omit*)
79 *tongue and belly* Tongue and entrails were left for the gods in ancient sacrifices
    (Lucas).
81 *throughly* thoroughly
82 *too* Qq2–4 (to Q1)

BOSOLA

   [*Aside*] Mercy upon me, what a fatal judgment

   Hath fall'n upon this Ferdinand!

PESCARA   Knows your Grace

   What accident hath brought unto the Prince   85

   This strange distraction?

CARDINAL

   [*Aside*] I must feign somewhat. Thus they say it grew:

   You have heard it rumour'd for these many years,

   None of our family dies, but there is seen

   The shape of an old woman, which is given   90

   By tradition, to us, to have been murther'd

   By her nephews, for her riches. Such a figure

   One night, as the Prince sat up late at's book,

   Appear'd to him; when crying out for help,

   The gentlemen of's chamber found his Grace   95

   All on a cold sweat, alter'd much in face

   And language. Since which apparition

   He hath grown worse and worse, and I much fear

   He cannot live.

BOSOLA

   Sir, I would speak with you.

PESCARA   We'll leave your Grace,   100

   Wishing to the sick Prince, our noble lord,

   All health of mind and body.

CARDINAL   You are most welcome.

           [*Exeunt* PESCARA, MALATESTE *and* DOCTOR]

   [*Aside*] Are you come? So: this fellow must not know

   By any means I had intelligence

   In our Duchess' death. For, though I counsell'd it,   105

   The full of all the'engagement seem'd to grow

   From Ferdinand. Now sir, how fares our sister?

   I do not think but sorrow makes her look

   Like to an oft-dy'd garment. She shall now

   Taste comfort from me: why do you look so wildly?   110

   Oh, the fortune of your master here, the Prince

   Dejects you, but be you of happy comfort:

   If you'll do one thing for me I'll entreat,

   Though he had a cold tombstone o'er his bones,

   I'll'd make you what you would be.

BOSOLA   Any thing;   115

---

106 *The ... engagement* the complete scope of Bosola's engagement to act as
    intelligencer; *engagement* Q1 (agreement Qq2–4)
115 *you would* Q1 (you should Qq2–3; you'd Q4)

Give it me in a breath, and let me fly to't:
They that think long, small expedition win,
For musing much o'th' end, cannot begin.

[*Enter* JULIA]

JULIA
Sir, will you come in to supper?
CARDINAL   I am busy, leave me.
JULIA [*Aside*]
What an excellent shape hath that fellow!   *Exit.*   120
CARDINAL
'Tis thus: Antonio lurks here in Milan;
Inquire him out, and kill him: while he lives
Our sister cannot marry, and I have thought
Of an excellent match for her: do this, and style me
Thy advancement.
BOSOLA   But by what means shall I find him out?   125
CARDINAL
There is a gentleman, call'd Delio
Here in the camp, that hath been long approv'd
His loyal friend. Set eye upon that fellow,
Follow him to mass; may be Antonio,
Although he do account religion   130
But a school-name, for fashion of the world,
May accompany him: or else go inquire out
Delio's confessor, and see if you can bribe
Him to reveal it: there are a thousand ways
A man might find to trace him: as, to know   135
What fellows haunt the Jews for taking up
Great sums of money, for sure he's in want;
Or else go to th' picture-makers, and learn

---

116 *it me* Q1, Q4 (me it Qq2–3)

125 *But by* Q1 (By Qq2–4)

127 *the camp* i.e. in Milan: a reminder that the Cardinal has turned soldier and
that, to him and his brother, real military action is preferred to the 'sportive
action' in which Antonio excelled. See II.ii.9–10.
    approv'd proved, confirmed

132–34 Not only is the Cardinal himself irreligious; he expects lesser churchmen
to be like him, and as open to corruption as he is.

138–39 Webster's familiarity with portrait painters in the immediate neigh-
bourhood of his family's business may lie behind these lines (Forker, pp.
19–20).

Who brought her picture lately: some of these
Happily may take –
BOSOLA   Well, I'll not freeze i'th' business,   140
I would see that wretched thing, Antonio,
Above all sights i'th' world.
CARDINAL   Do, and be happy.   *Exit.*
BOSOLA
This fellow doth breed basilisks in's eyes,
He's nothing else but murder: yet he seems
Not to have notice of the Duchess' death.   145
'Tis his cunning: I must follow his example;
There cannot be a surer way to trace,
Than that of an old fox.

[*Enter* JULIA *with a pistol*]

JULIA   So, sir, you are well met.
BOSOLA
How now?
JULIA   Nay, the doors are fast enough.
Now sir, I will make you confess your treachery.   150
BOSOLA
Treachery?
JULIA   Yes, confess to me
Which of my women 'twas you hir'd, to put
Love-powder into my drink?
BOSOLA   Love-powder?

139 *brought* Qq1–3, Sampson, Gunby (Q4 *omits*; bought Dyce, Hazlitt,
      Vaughan, McIlwraith, Brown). Lucas, who reads [bought], noted in his
      1958 edition that *picture-makers* might also be dealers to whom Antonio
      could sell a miniature of the Duchess. Moreover, one has to assume that
      the Duchess's picture was normally on sale in Milan (p. 215). It could be
      added that Antonio is still hoping to be reunited with his wife and might
      not need a picture to remind himself of her.
140 *Happily* haply
142 *Do ... happy.* Assuming that Bosola has spoken sarcastically, the Cardinal
      responds in the same tone.
143 *basilisks* See III.ii.88n.
148 s.d. ed. (*Enter Julia, pointing a pistol at him* Lucas)
150 ff. Although this passage eases dramatic tension by providing comic relief
      as Bosola and Julia speak at cross-purposes, its structural function is to
      present an ironic parallel to the Duchess's wooing of Antonio. The contrary
      view – that the parallel diminishes the Duchess through parody – is advanced
      by Joyce E. Paterson in *Curs'd Example*, pp. 89–95.
151–55 Cf. III.i.63–69.

JULIA

  Yes, when I was at Malfi;

  Why should I fall in love with such a face else?   155

  I have already suffer'd for thee so much pain,

  The only remedy to do me good

  Is to kill my longing.

BOSOLA   Sure, your pistol holds

  Nothing but perfumes or kissing-comfits: excellent lady,

  You have a pretty way on't to discover   160

  Your longing. Come, come, I'll disarm you

  And arm you thus: [*Embraces her*] yet this is wondrous

                                   strange.

JULIA

  Compare thy form and my eyes together,

  You'll find my love no such great miracle.

  [*Kisses him*] Now you'll say   165

  I am a wanton. This nice modesty in ladies

  Is but a troublesome familiar

  That haunts them.

BOSOLA

  Know you me, I am a blunt soldier.

JULIA   The better: 170

  Sure, there wants fire where there are no lively sparks

  Of roughness.

BOSOLA   And I want compliment.

JULIA   Why, ignorance

  In courtship cannot make you do amiss,

  If you have a heart to do well.

BOSOLA   You are very fair.

JULIA

  Nay, if you lay beauty to my charge,

  I must plead unguilty.

BOSOLA   Your bright eyes   175

  Carry a quiver of darts in them, sharper

  Than sunbeams.

JULIA   You will mar me with commendation,

  Put yourself to the charge of courting me,

  Whereas now I woo you.

---

159 *kissing-comfits* comfits used to sweeten the breath
162 *arm* embrace. Cf. I.ii.384.
167 *familiar* familiar spirit
171 *want compliment* am lacking in complimentary language
179 *woo* ed. (woe Qq1–2, Q4; wo Q3)

BOSOLA

  [*Aside*] I have it, I will work upon this creature,   180
  Let us grow most amorously familiar.
  If the great Cardinal now should see me thus,
  Would he not count me a villain?

JULIA

  No, he might count me a wanton,
  Not lay a scruple of offence on you: 185
  For if I see, and steal a diamond,
  The fault is not i'th' stone, but in me the thief
  That purloins it. I am sudden with you;
  We that are great women of pleasure, use to cut off
  These uncertain wishes and unquiet longings,   190
  And in an instant join the sweet delight
  And the pretty excuse together: had you been i'th' street,
  Under my chamber window, even there
  I should have courted you.

BOSOLA   Oh, you are an excellent lady.

JULIA

  Bid me do somewhat for you presently   195
  To express I love you.

BOSOLA   I will, and if you love me,
  Fail not to effect it.
  The Cardinal is grown wondrous melancholy,
  Demand the cause, let him not put you off
  With feign'd excuse; discover the main ground on't.   200

JULIA

  Why would you know this?

BOSOLA   I have depended on him,
  And I hear that he is fall'n in some disgrace
  With the Emperor: if he be, like the mice
  That forsake falling houses, I would shift
  To other dependence.   205

JULIA

  You shall not need follow the wars:
  I'll be your maintenance.

BOSOLA

  And I your loyal servant;
  But I cannot leave my calling.

JULIA   Not leave an

185 *scruple* a minute amount
193 *Under . . . there* Q1 (Qq2–4 *omit*)
195 *presently* immediately
206 *shall not* Qq1–2, Q4 (shall Q3)
209 *my* Qq 1–2, Q4 (your Q3)

Ungrateful general for the love of a sweet lady?   210
You are like some, cannot sleep in feather-beds,
But must have blocks for their pillows.
BOSOLA   Will you do this?
JULIA
Cunningly.
BOSOLA   Tomorrow I'll expect th'intelligence.
JULIA
Tomorrow? get you into my cabinet,
You shall have it with you: do not delay me,   215
No more than I do you. I am like one
That is condemn'd: I have my pardon promis'd,
But I would see it seal'd. Go, get you in,
You shall see me wind my tongue about his heart
Like a skein of silk.   220

[BOSOLA *withdraws behind the traverse; enter* CARDINAL]

CARDINAL
Where are you?

[*Enter* SERVANTS]

SERVANTS   Here.
CARDINAL   Let none upon your lives
Have conference with the Prince Ferdinand,
Unless I know it. [*Aside*] In this distraction
He may reveal the murther.   [*Exeunt* SERVANTS]
Yond's my ling'ring consumption: 225
I am weary of her; and by any means
Would be quit of –
JULIA   How now, my Lord?
What ails you?
CARDINAL   Nothing.
JULIA   Oh, you are much alter'd:
Come, I must be your secretary, and remove
This lead from off your bosom; what's the matter?   230
CARDINAL
I may not tell you.
JULIA   Are you so far in love with sorrow,
You cannot part with part of it? or think you
I cannot love your Grace when you are sad,

---

227 *quit of* – ed. (quit off Qq1–2; quit off her Qq3–4; quit of   Dyce, Hazlitt,
     Vaughan, McIlwraith, Brown). Lucas, with Sampson, retains Q1 reading
     but suggests that 'quite off' may be possible.
229 *secretary* **confidant**

As well as merry? or do you suspect
I, that have been a secret to your heart   235
These many winters, cannot be the same
Unto your tongue?
CARDINAL   Satisfy thy longing.
The only way to make thee keep my counsel
Is not to tell thee.
JULIA   Tell your echo this,
Or flatterers, that, like echoes, still report   240
What they hear, though most imperfect, and not me:
For, if that you be true unto yourself,
I'll know.
CARDINAL   Will you rack me?
JULIA   No, judgment shall
Draw it from you. It is an equal fault,
To tell one's secrets unto all, or none.   245
CARDINAL
The first argues folly.
JULIA   But the last tyranny.
CARDINAL
Very well; why, imagine I have committed
Some secret deed which I desire the world
May never hear of!
JULIA   Therefore may not I know it?
You have conceal'd for me as great a sin   250
As adultery. Sir, never was occasion
For perfect trial of my constancy
Till now. Sir, I beseech you.
CARDINAL   You'll repent it.
JULIA   Never.
CARDINAL
It hurries thee to ruin: I'll not tell thee.
Be well advis'd, and think what danger 'tis   255
To receive a prince's secrets: they that do,
Had need have their breasts hoop'd with adamant
To contain them. I pray thee yet be satisfi'd,
Examine thine own frailty; 'tis more easy
To tie knots, than unloose them: 'tis a secret   260
That, like a ling'ring poison, may chance lie
Spread in thy veins, and kill thee seven year hence.
JULIA
Now you dally with me.
CARDINAL   No more; thou shalt know it.
By my appointment the great Duchess of Malfi

251 *Sir . . . occasion* Q1 (Sir, I beseech you Qq2–4)

And two of her young children, four nights since 265
Were strangled.

JULIA   Oh Heaven! Sir, what have you done?

CARDINAL
How now? how settles this? Think you your bosom
Will be a grave dark and obscure enough
For such a secret?

JULIA   You have undone yourself, sir.

CARDINAL
Why?

JULIA   It lies not in me to conceal it.

CARDINAL   No? 270
Come, I will swear you to't upon this book.

JULIA
Most religiously.

CARDINAL   Kiss it.   [*She kisses a Bible*]
Now you shall never utter it; thy curiosity
Hath undone thee; thou'rt poison'd with that book.
Because I knew thou couldst not keep my counsel, 275
I have bound thee to't by death.

[*Enter* BOSOLA]

BOSOLA
For pity-sake, hold.

CARDINAL   Ha, Bosola!

JULIA   I forgive you
This equal piece of justice you have done:
For I betray'd your counsel to that fellow;
He overheard it; that was the cause I said 280
It lay not in me to conceal it.

BOSOLA   Oh foolish woman,
Couldst not thou have poison'd him?

JULIA   'Tis weakness,
Too much to think what should have been done. I go,
I know not whither.   [*Dies*]

CARDINAL   Wherefore com'st thou hither?

BOSOLA
That I might find a great man, like yourself, 285
Not out of his wits, as the Lord Ferdinand,
To remember my service.

CARDINAL   I'll have thee hew'd in pieces.

---

267 *how settles this?* 'A figure drawn from the settling of liquid, hence its clarifying;
as if the Cardinal now saw the situation more clearly' (Sampson).

BOSOLA

Make not yourself such a promise of that life
Which is not yours to dispose of.

CARDINAL   Who plac'd thee here?

BOSOLA

Her lust, as she intended.

CARDINAL   Very well;   290
Now you know me for your fellow murderer.

BOSOLA

And wherefore should you lay fair marble colours
Upon your rotten purposes to me?
Unless you imitate some that do plot great treasons,
And when they have done, go hide themselves i'th' graves   295
Of those were actors in't.

CARDINAL

No more: there is a fortune attends thee.

BOSOLA

Shall I go sue to Fortune any longer?
'Tis the fool's pilgrimage.

CARDINAL   I have honours in store for thee.

BOSOLA

There are a many ways that conduct to seeming   300
Honour, and some of them very dirty ones.

CARDINAL

Throw to the devil
Thy melancholy; the fire burns well,
What need we keep a stirring of't, and make
A greater smother? Thou wilt kill Antonio?   305

BOSOLA

Yes.

CARDINAL   Take up that body.

BOSOLA   I think I shall
Shortly grow the common bier for churchyards!

CARDINAL

I will allow thee some dozen of attendants,
To aid thee in the murther.

BOSOLA   Oh, by no means: physicians that apply horse-   310
leeches to any rank swelling, use to cut off their tails, that

292–93 'Why give the crumbling and corrupt fabric of your purposes the appear-
      ance of marble's strength and beauty for my benefit?'
298 *to Fortune* ed. (to fortune Q1; a fortune Qq2–3; a Fortune Q4)
300 *a many* Q1 (many Qq2–4)
305 *greater* Q1 (great Qq2–4)
307 *bier* Qq3–4 (beare Qq1–2)
311 *off* Q3 (of Qq1–2; Q4 *omits*)

the blood may run through them the faster. Let me have no
train, when I go to shed blood, lest it make me have a greater,
when I ride to the gallows.

CARDINAL

Come to me after midnight, to help to remove that body   315
To her own lodging. I'll give out she di'd o'th' plague;
'Twill breed the less inquiry after her death.

BOSOLA

Where's Castruchio her husband?

CARDINAL

He's rode to Naples to take possession
Of Antonio's citadel.   320

BOSOLA

Believe me, you have done a very happy turn.

CARDINAL

Fail not to come. There is the master-key
Of our lodgings: and by that you may conceive
What trust I plant in you.   *Exit.*

BOSOLA   You shall find me ready.
Oh poor Antonio, though nothing be so needful   325
To thy estate, as pity, yet I find
Nothing so dangerous. I must look to my footing;
In such slippery ice-pavements men had need
To be frost-nail'd well: they may break their necks else.
The president's here afore me: how this man   330
Bears up in blood! seems fearless! Why, 'tis well:
Security some men call the suburbs of hell,
Only a dead wall between. Well, good Antonio,
I'll seek thee out; and all my care shall be
To put thee into safety from the reach   335
Of these most cruel biters, that have got
Some of thy blood already. It may be,
I'll join with thee in a most just revenge.
The weakest arm is strong enough, that strikes
With the sword of justice. Still methinks the Duchess   340

319 *rode* Qq2–4 (rod Q1)

330 *president* precedent

331 *bears up in blood* 'keeps up his courage' (Lucas); 'persists, or drives forward,
in shedding blood' (Brown)

332 *security* over-confidence. Gunby notes that, to theologians, 'spiritual' security comprised an undue confidence in the certainty of salvation; 'carnal'
security – seen by Bosola in the Cardinal – a dangerous concentration on
mortal life and indifference to the immortal (p. 445).

333 *dead* (1) inert; (2) unbroken. Cf. V.v.96.

336 *biters* sheep-biters. Cf. V.ii.51n.

Haunts me: there, there: 'tis nothing but my melancholy.
O penitence, let me truly taste thy cup,
That throws men down, only to raise them up.   *Exit.*

Scene iii

[*Enter* ANTONIO *and* DELIO; *there is an*] ECHO (*from the*
DUCHESS' *grave*).

DELIO
Yond's the Cardinal's window. This fortification
Grew from the ruins of an ancient abbey:
And to yond side o'th' river lies a wall,
Piece of a cloister, which in my opinion
Gives the best echo that you ever heard;   5
So hollow, and so dismal, and withal
So plain in the distinction of our words,
That many have suppos'd it is a spirit
That answers.
ANTONIO   I do love these ancient ruins:
We never tread upon them, but we set   10
Our foot upon some reverend history,
And, questionless, here in this open court,
Which now lies naked to the injuries
Of stormy weather, some men lie interr'd
Lov'd the church so well, and gave so largely to't,   15
They thought it should have canopi'd their bones
Till doomsday. But all things have their end:
Churches and cities, which have diseases like to men
Must have like death that we have.
ECHO   *Like death that we have.*
DELIO
Now the echo hath caught you.
ANTONIO   It groan'd, methought, and gave   20

---

343 *raise* Q1, Qq3–4 (rise Q3)
Act V, Scene iii 'This is perhaps the most purely moving scene the Duchess has'
(Charles Williams, 'On the Poetry of *The Duchess of Malfi*', Sylvan Press edition,
London, 1945, p. xxi). See also Lucas II, 195–96 and Michael Neill, 'Monuments
and ruins as symbols in *The Duchess of Malfi*', *TD* 4 (1982), 71–87. Robert C.
Jones, in 'Italian Settings and the "World" of Elizabethan Tragedy', *SEL* 10
(1970), 251–68, points out that 'Ruined abbeys and the secular buildings that
grew up in their midst were, after Henry VIII, an English phenomenon, not an
Italian one' (p. 264).
14 *men* Q1 (Qq2–4 *omit*)

A very deadly accent!

ECHO   *Deadly accent.*

DELIO

I told you 'twas a pretty one. You may make it
A huntsman, or a falconer, a musician
Or a thing of sorrow.

ECHO   *A thing of sorrow.*

ANTONIO

Ay sure: that suits it best.

ECHO   *That suits it best.*   25

ANTONIO

'Tis very like my wife's voice.

ECHO   *Ay, wife's voice.*

DELIO

Come: let's walk farther from't:
I would not have you go to th' Cardinal's tonight:
Do not.

ECHO   *Do not.*

DELIO

Wisdom doth not more moderate wasting sorrow   30
Than time: take time for't: be mindful of thy safety.

ECHO

Be mindful of thy safety.

ANTONIO   Necessity compels me:
Make scrutiny throughout the passages
Of your own life; you'll find it impossible
To fly your fate.

ECHO   *O fly your fate.*   35

DELIO

Hark: the dead stones seem to have pity on you
And give you good counsel.

ANTONIO   Echo, I will not talk with thee;
For thou art a dead thing.

ECHO   *Thou art a dead thing.*

ANTONIO

My Duchess is asleep now,
And her little ones, I hope sweetly: oh Heaven   40
Shall I never see her more?

ECHO   *Never see her more.*

---

27 *let's* Q4 (let's us Qq1–3)
28 *go* Q1b, Q4 (too Q1a; Qq2–3 *omit*)
33 *passages* Q4 (passes Qq1–3)
35 s.p. ed. *Ecc.* Q4 (Qq1–3 *omit*)
40–41 See III.v.79–80n.
41 The line recalls Antonio's words at III.v.81–83.

ANTONIO

I mark'd not one repetition of the Echo
But that: and on the sudden, a clear light
Presented me a face folded in sorrow.

DELIO

Your fancy; merely.

ANTONIO   Come: I'll be out of this ague;   45
For to live thus, is not indeed to live:
It is a mockery, and abuse of life.
I will not henceforth save myself by halves;
Lose all, or nothing.

DELIO   Your own virtue save you.
I'll fetch your eldest son; and second you: 50
It may be that the sight of his own blood
Spread in so sweet a figure, may beget
The more compassion.

ANTONIO   However, fare you well.
Though in our miseries Fortune hath a part
Yet, in our noble sufferings, she hath none: 55
Contempt of pain, that we may call our own.   *Exe[unt]*.

Scene iv

[*Enter*] CARDINAL, PESCARA, MALATESTE, RODERIGO, GRISOLAN

CARDINAL

You shall not watch tonight by the sick Prince;
His Grace is very well recover'd.

MALATESTE

Good my lord, suffer us.

CARDINAL   Oh, by no means:
The noise and change of object in his eye
Doth more distract him. I pray, all to bed,   5
And though you hear him in his violent fit,

52 *in* Q1 (into Qq2–4)
53 s.p. ed. (Qq *omit*) Lucas noted that the speech 'begins on a fresh line . . . as
    if there were a fresh speaker; and the stoic words . . . come better from
    Antonio than as a preachment to him from Delio' (Lucas II, 210).
Act V, Scene iv The scene takes place at night. Despite the different stage
conditions at the Blackfriars and the Globe, both audiences would have under-
stood Bosola's confusion when he is alone with Antonio, who has no lantern.
McLuskie and Uglow point out that 'darkness was indicated as much by props
and dialogue as by any physical change' (p. 11). The lantern reminds us of the
previous encounter between Antonio and Bosola in darkness, in II.iii.

Do not rise, I entreat you.

PESCARA   So sir, we shall not –

CARDINAL

Nay, I must have you promise
Upon your honours, for I was enjoin'd to't
By himself; and he seem'd to urge it sensibly.   10

PESCARA

Let our honours bind this trifle.

CARDINAL

Nor any of your followers.

PESCARA   Neither.

CARDINAL

It may be to make trial of your promise
When he's asleep, myself will rise, and feign
Some of his mad tricks, and cry out for help,   15
And feign myself in danger.

MALATESTE   If your throat were cutting,
I'll'd not come at you, now I have protested against it.

CARDINAL

Why, I thank you.   [*Withdraws*]

GRISOLAN   'Twas a foul storm tonight.

RODERIGO

The Lord Ferdinand's chamber shook like an osier.

MALATESTE

'Twas nothing but pure kindness in the devil,   20
To rock his own child.   *Exeunt* [RODERIGO,
                    MALATESTE, PESCARA, GRISOLAN].

CARDINAL

The reason why I would not suffer these
About my brother, is because at midnight
I may with better privacy convey
Julia's body to her own lodging. O, my conscience!   25
I would pray now: but the devil takes away my heart
For having any confidence in prayer.
About this hour I appointed Bosola
To fetch the body: when he hath serv'd my turn,
He dies.   *Exit.*   30

[*Enter* BOSOLA]

BOSOLA

Ha! 'twas the Cardinal's voice. I heard him name
Bosola, and my death: listen, I hear one's footing.

[*Enter* FERDINAND]

11 *our* Qq2–4 (out Q1)

FERDINAND

Strangling is a very quiet death.

BOSOLA

Nay then I see, I must stand upon my guard.

FERDINAND

What say' to that? Whisper, softly: do you agree to't?   35
So it must be done i'th' dark: the Cardinal
Would not for a thousand pounds the doctor should see it.

Exit.

BOSOLA

My death is plotted; here's the consequence of murther.
We value not desert, nor Christian breath,
When we know black deeds must be cur'd with death. [*Withdraws*]   40

[*Enter* ANTONIO *and a* SERVANT]

SERVANT

Here stay sir, and be confident, I pray:
I'll fetch you a dark lanthorn.   *Exit.*

ANTONIO   Could I take him

At his prayers, there were hope of pardon.

BOSOLA

Fall right my sword: [*Strikes* ANTONIO *down from behind*]
I'll not give thee so much leisure as to pray.   45

ANTONIO

Oh, I am gone. Thou hast ended a long suit,
In a minute.

BOSOLA   What are thou?

ANTONIO   A most wretched thing

That only have thy benefit in death,
To appear myself.

[*Enter* SERVANT *with a dark lanthorn*]

SERVANT   Where are you sir?

ANTONIO

Very near my home. Bosola?

SERVANT   Oh misfortune!   50

33 *quiet* Qq2–4 (quiein Q1)

35 *say'* Qq1–2 (say you Qq3–4)

42 *dark lanthorn* Cf. II.iii.1 s.d. note.

42–45 These lines contain interesting echoes of *Hamlet* III.iii.36–97. Antonio
    hopes to find the Cardinal praying and, presumably, more disposed to grant
    him a Christian pardon than when in his martial frame of mind. Bosola, as
    Lucas suggests, mistakes Antonio's voice for that of 'some cut-throat who
    hopes to get a pardon from the Cardinal in return for murdering the
    inconvenient Bosola' (Lucas II, 196–97). In this case the assailant, unlike
    Hamlet, would strangle his victim as he prays.

BOSOLA

[*To* SERVANT] Smother thy pity, thou art dead else. Antonio!
The man I would have sav'd 'bove mine own life!
We are merely the stars' tennis-balls, struck and banded
Which way please them: oh good Antonio,
I'll whisper one thing in thy dying ear,   55
Shall make thy heart break quickly. Thy fair Duchess
And two sweet children –

ANTONIO   Their very names

Kindle a little life in me.

BOSOLA   Are murder'd!

ANTONIO

Some men have wish'd to die
At the hearing of sad tidings: I am glad   60
That I shall do't in sadness: I would not now
Wish my wounds balm'd, nor heal'd: for I have no use
To put my life to. In all our quest of greatness,
Like wanton boys, whose pastime is their care,
We follow after bubbles, blown in th'air.   65
Pleasure of life, what is't? only the good hours
Of an ague: merely a preparative to rest,
To endure vexation. I do not ask
The process of my death: only commend me
To Delio.

BOSOLA   Break, heart!   70

ANTONIO

---

53 *banded* bandied

53–54 Brown notes (p. 164) that this is a familiar conceit, found in Plautus, Florio and Sidney's *Arcadia*. Peter Ure suggested a more immediate source, for Webster, in Sir William Alexander's *The Alexandrean Tragedy* V.i.2577–78: 'I thinke the world is but a Tenis-Court,/ Where Fortune doth play States, tosse men for Balls' ('*The Duchess of Malfi*: Another Debt to Sir William Alexander', *N&Q* n.s. 13 (1966), p. 296). In 'Two Notes upon Emblems and the English Renaissance Drama', *N&Q* n.s. 18 (1971), 28–29, S. Schuman points out that Peacham's emblem 'Sic Nos Dii' in *Minerva Britanna* (1612), p. 113, has a verse closer to Webster, i.e.: 'So when the Gods alone, have struck vs low,/ (For men as balls, within their hands are said,)/ We chiefly then, should manly courage show,/ And not for every trifle be afraid'.

60 *sad tidings* Brereton had 'a sort of suspicion that we should read "glad tidings"' (p. 15) which Lucas shared (Lucas II, 197).

61 *sadness* seriousness

63–65 In 'Webster's "wanton boyes"', *N&Q* n.s. 2 (1955), 294–95, Inga-Stina Ekeblad indicates that the image is not an echo of *King Lear* IV.i.37–38; it derives from an emblem found in Whitney's *A Choice of Emblemes* (1586) and Hadrianus Junius's collection of emblemata.

65 *in th'* Q1 (i'th' Qq2–4)

And let my son fly the courts of princes.   [*Dies*]

BOSOLA

Thou seem'st to have lov'd Antonio?

SERVANT   I brought him hither,

To have reconcil'd him to the Cardinal.

BOSOLA

I do not ask thee that.

Take him up, if thou tender thine own life,   75

And bear him where the Lady Julia

Was wont to lodge. Oh, my fate moves swift.

I have this Cardinal in the forge already,

Now I'll bring him to th' hammer. (O direful misprision!)

I will not imitate things glorious,   80

No more than base: I'll be mine own example.

On, on: and look thou represent, for silence,

The thing thou bear'st.   *Exeunt.*

Scene v

[*Enter*] CARDINAL *(with a book)*

CARDINAL

I am puzzl'd in a question about hell:

He says, in hell there's one material fire,

And yet it shall not burn all men alike.

Lay him by. How tedious is a guilty conscience!

When I look into the fishponds, in my garden,   5

Methinks I see a thing arm'd with a rake

That seems to strike at me. Now? Art thou come?

[*Enter* BOSOLA *and* SERVANT *with* ANTONIO'S *body*]

73 *to the* Q1 (with the Qq2–4)
74 *ask thee* want thee to do
75 *tender* value
79 *misprision* mistake
1 s.d. Brown notes that a book was 'an old stage-device for indicating melancholy or introspection' (p. 166). It was obviously a theological work which the Cardinal was consulting.
5–7 R.K.R. Thornton, in 'The Cardinal's Rake in *The Duchess of Malfi*' *N&Q* n.s. 16 (1969), 295–96, compares the image with William Bullein's *A Dialogue against the Fever Pestilence* (1564, 1573, 1578) where a husband interprets for his wife a picture of a man who, with a golden-toothed rake, stoops in the lake, as one who 'raketh with the Deuils golden rake, euen in the conscience of the coueitous patrons or compounders hart, which geueth the benefice . . .' Thus the Cardinal's rake symbolizes his sin of simony and worldliness, not the weapon that kills him.

    Thou look'st ghastly:
    There sits in thy face some great determination,
    Mix'd with some fear.
BOSOLA   Thus it lightens into action: 10
    I am come to kill thee.
CARDINAL   Ha? Help! our guard!
BOSOLA
    Thou art deceiv'd:
    They are out of thy howling.
CARDINAL
    Hold: and I will faithfully divide
    Revenues with thee.
BOSOLA   Thy prayers and proffers   15
    Are both unseasonable.
CARDINAL   Raise the watch:
    We are betray'd!
BOSOLA   I have confin'd your flight:
    I'll suffer your retreat to Julia's chamber,
    But no further.
CARDINAL   Help: we are betray'd!

     [*Enter* PESCARA, MALATESTE, RODERIGO *and* GRISOLAN, *above*]

MALATESTE   Listen.
CARDINAL
    My dukedom for rescue!
RODERIGO   Fie upon his counterfeiting.   20
MALATESTE
    Why, 'tis not the Cardinal.
RODERIGO   Yes, yes, 'tis he:
    But I'll see him hang'd, ere I'll go down to him.
CARDINAL
    Here's a plot upon me; I am assaulted. I am lost,
    Unless some rescue!
GRISOLAN   He doth this pretty well:
    But it will not serve to laugh me out of mine honour.   25
CARDINAL
    The sword's at my throat!
RODERIGO   You would not bawl so loud then.

---

  10 *lightens* flashes out into
  14 *and* Q1 (Qq2–4 *omit*)
  14–16 Bosola's refusal of wealth stresses the change in his character and the
     strength of his determination to do something worth his dejection (IV.ii.367–
     69).

MALATESTE
    Come, come: let's go to bed: he told us thus much
                               aforehand.
PESCARA
    He wish'd you should not come at him: but believe't,
    The accent of the voice sounds not in jest.
    I'll down to him, howsoever, and with engines   30
    Force ope the doors.   [*Exit*]
RODERIGO   Let's follow him aloof,
    And note how the Cardinal will laugh at him. [*Exeunt above*]
BOSOLA
    There's for you first:
    'Cause you shall not unbarricade the door
    To let in rescue.   *He kills the* SERVANT.   35
CARDINAL
    What cause hast thou to pursue my life?
BOSOLA   Look there.
CARDINAL
    Antonio!
BOSOLA   Slain by my hand unwittingly.
    Pray, and be sudden: when thou kill'd'st thy sister,
    Thou took'st from Justice her most equal balance,
    And left her naught but her sword.
CARDINAL   O mercy!   40
BOSOLA
    Now it seems thy greatness was only outward:
    For thou fall'st faster of thyself than calamity
    Can drive thee. I'll not waste longer time. There.
                   [*Stabs the* CARDINAL]
CARDINAL
    Thou hast hurt me.
BOSOLA   Again.   [*Stabs him again*]
CARDINAL   Shall I die like a leveret
    Without any resistance? Help, help, help!   45
    I am slain.

                [*Enter* FERDINAND]

FERDINAND Th'alarum? give me a fresh horse.
    Rally the vaunt-guard; or the day is lost.

27 *let's* Qq2–4 (lets's Q1)
30 *engines* tools, instruments
40 *her sword* Q1 (the sword Qq2–4)
44 *leveret* young hare, considered too feeble to be worth hunting (Brown)
47 *vaunt-guard* vanguard

Yield, yield! I give you the honour of arms,
Shake my sword over you, will you yield?

CARDINAL

Help me, I am your brother.

FERDINAND   The devil?   50
My brother fight upon the adverse party?

> *He wounds the* CARDINAL *and (in the scuffle)*
> *gives* BOSOLA *his death wound.*

There flies your ransom.

CARDINAL   Oh Justice:
I suffer now for what hath former bin
Sorrow is held the eldest child of sin.

FERDINAND   Now you're brave fellows. Caesar's fortune   55
was harder than Pompey's: Caesar died in the arms of
prosperity, Pompey at the feet of disgrace: you both
died in the field, the pain's nothing. Pain many times is
taken away with the apprehension of greater, as the tooth-
ache with the sight of a barber that comes to pull it out: 60
there's philosophy for you.

BOSOLA

Now my revenge is perfect: sink, thou main cause
Of my undoing: the last part of my life
Hath done me best service.   *He kills* FERDINAND.

FERDINAND

Give me some wet hay, I am broken winded.   65
I do account this world but a dog-kennel:
I will vault credit, and affect high pleasures
Beyond death.

BOSOLA   He seems to come to himself,
Now he's so near the bottom.

FERDINAND

My sister, oh! my sister, there's the cause on't.   70
Whether we fall by ambition, blood, or lust,
Like diamonds we are cut with our own dust.   [*Dies*]

48–52 At first Ferdinand offers his adversary *the honour of arms* – i.e. the chance
of being taken prisoner with the prospect of being ransomed – but then
changes his mind and decides to press home his advantage to the death.

50 *The devil?* Qq, Lucas, Gunby (The devil! Dyce, Hazlitt, Sampson,
Vaughan, McIlwraith, Brown). A query implies Ferdinand's identification
of the Cardinal and the devil; an exclamation mark implies a curse. Cf. note
on III.v.1.

51 s.d. in the margin, opposite ll. 51–52a–b in Qq

53 *bin* Qq1–3 (been Q4)

68 *Beyond death* Q1 (Qq2–4 *omit*)

CARDINAL
  Thou hast thy payment too.
BOSOLA
  Yes, I hold my weary soul in my teeth;
  'Tis ready to part from me. I do glory   75
  That thou, which stood'st like a huge pyramid
  Begun upon a large and ample base,
  Shalt end in a little point, a kind of nothing.

        [*Enter* PESCARA, MALATESTE, RODERIGO *and* GRISOLAN]

PESCARA
  How now, my lord?
MALATESTE   O sad disaster!
RODERIGO   How comes this?
BOSOLA
  Revenge, for the Duchess of Malfi, murdered   80
  By th' Aragonian brethren; for Antonio,
  Slain by this hand; for lustful Julia,
  Poison'd by this man; and lastly, for myself,
  That was an actor in the main of all,
  Much 'gainst mine own good nature, yet i'th' end   85
  Neglected.
PESCARA   How now, my lord?
CARDINAL   Look to my brother:
  He gave us these large wounds, as we were struggling
  Here i'th'rushes. And now, I pray, let me
  Be laid by, and never thought of.   [*Dies*]
PESCARA
  How fatally, it seems, he did withstand   90
  His own rescue!
MALATESTE   Thou wretched thing of blood,
  How came Antonio by his death?
BOSOLA
  In a mist: I know not how;
  Such a mistake as I have often seen
  In a play. Oh, I am gone: 95
  We are only like dead walls, or vaulted graves
  That, ruin'd, yields no echo. Fare you well;
  It may be pain: but no harm to me to die
  In so good a quarrel. Oh this gloomy world,

76–79 See Additional Notes, p. 136.
82 *this* Q4 (his Qq1–3)
88 *rushes* Green rushes were strewn on both the floors of private apartments
      and stages of public theatres (Brown).
96 *dead* (1) inert; (2) unbroken. Cf. V.ii.333 n.

In what a shadow, or deep pit of darkness   100
Doth, womanish, and fearful, mankind live?
Let worthy minds ne'er stagger in distrust
To suffer death or shame for what is just:
Mine is another voyage.   [*Dies*]

PESCARA
The noble Delio, as I came to th'palace,   105
Told me of Antonio's being here, and show'd me
A pretty gentleman his son and heir.

[*Enter* DELIO *with* ANTONIO'S *son*]

MALATESTE
O sir, you come too late.

DELIO   I heard so, and
Was arm'd for't ere I came. Let us make noble use
Of this great ruin; and join all our force   110
To establish this young hopeful gentleman
In's mother's right. These wretched eminent things
Leave no more fame behind 'em, than should one
Fall in a frost, and leave his print in snow,
As soon as the sun shines, it ever melts   115
Both form and matter. I have ever thought
Nature doth nothing so great for great men,
As when she's pleas'd to make them lords of truth:
Integrity of life is fame's best friend,
Which nobly, beyond death, shall crown the end.   *Exeunt.*   120

FINIS

99–104, 119–20 See Additional Notes, pp. 136–37.

ADDITIONAL NOTES

I.ii.30 *children of Israel.* According to *OED* the name Ismaelite was formerly given (especially by the Jews) to the Arabs as descendants of Ishmael, Abraham's son by the bondwoman Hagar. (See Genesis 16.15–16; 17.18–27; 21.9–21; 25.12–18 and I Chronicles 1.29–30.) If the reading 'children of Ismael' is correct, Julia's pun refers simply to the Arabs as tent-dwellers. Despite this obvious meaning I suspect that we should read 'children of Israel'.

First, the spelling 'Ismael' was decidedly old-fashioned for a play printed in 1623. It was to be found in early sixteenth-century versions of the Bible such as Coverdale's (1535), 'Matthew's Bible' (1537) and Cranmer's (1540), and it was used in the Bishops' Bible of 1568; but the spelling 'Ishmael' was introduced in the Genevan version of 1560, and this version, which was reprinted some two hundred times, was far the most popular in Elizabethan England. The same spelling was retained in the King James (or 'Authorized') Version of 1611.

Secondly, although it might have been known that, especially among the Jews, Arabs were referred to as the children of Ishmael, there is no reference in the Old Testament itself to Ishmael or his descendants as tent-dwellers. On the contrary, in Genesis 25.16 reference is made to their towns and castles, and it was Jabal who, in Genesis 4.20, was called 'the father of such as dwell in tents'. There are, however, several Old Testament references to the Israelites or children of Israel, both individually and collectively, dwelling in tents. Among these Psalm 78.55 – 'He cast out the heathen also before them, and made the tribes of Israel to dwell in their tents' – and II Kings 13.5 – 'and the children of Israel dwelt in their tents, as aforetime' – might be cited as obvious bases of Julia's pun. I suggest, therefore, that Webster originally wrote Is*r*ael which, by scribal or compositorial error became Is*m*ael and thereby Julia's joke, though perfectly intelligible, lost some of its immediacy.

I.ii. 112–27 Antonio's speech is based on George Pettie's translation of Guazzo's *Civil Conversation,* ii (1581) I, 241–42: 'her talke and discourses are so delightfull, that you wyll only then beginne to bee sory, when shee endeth to speake: and wishe that shee woulde bee no more weary to speake, then you are to heare ... She wyll also in talke cast oft times upon a man such a sweete smyle, that it were enough to bryng him into a fooles Paradise, but that her countenance conteineth such continencie in it, as is sufficient to cut off all fond hope ... for conclusion I will say, that shee may well bee set for an

example, whereto other women ought to conforme them selves . . .'
(quoted by Dent, p. 184).

The Duchess of Malfi's Marriage

Two articles, not always in agreement on points of interpretation, which
throw light on the significance of marriages *Per verba de presenti* (I.ii.392)
and the contemporary attitude to them are: D.P. Harding's 'Elizabethan
Betrothals and *Measure for Measure*', *JEGP* 49 (1950), 139–58 and
Ernest Schanzer's 'The Marriage Contracts in *Measure for Measure*',
ShS 13 (1960), 81–89. For critical discussion of the significance of the
Duchess's marriage see F.W. Wadsworth, 'Webster's *Duchess of Malfi* in
the Light of Some Contemporary Ideas on Marriage and Remarriage',
PQ 35 (1956), 394–407; J.R. Mulryne, '*The White Devil* and *The Duchess
of Malfi*', *Jacobean Theatre*, edited by John Russell Brown and Bernard
Harris, *SUAS* 1 (1960), pp. 201–25 (especially pp. 219–22). A strong
expression of disapproval of the Duchess on the grounds of her choice
of marriage partner is voiced by Joyce E. Peterson in *Curs'd Example:
'The Duchess of Malfi' and Commonweal Tragedy*. More recently, Lisa
Jardine has indicated the threat to inheritance posed by a marriage like
the Duchess's: see *Still Harping on Daughters* (1983; 1989), pp. 68–102.

The evidence of history is, however, itself confusing. Brown reminds
us that, when *The Duchess of Malfi* was first performed 'Lady Arabella
Stuart lay imprisoned in the Tower for marrying Lord William Seymour,
a man who might strengthen her claim to James' throne' (Introduction,
p. xxxix). Forker points out that, though clandestine marriages were
often stringently punished, 'it is unreasonable to believe that popular
sympathy would be universally withheld' and 'despite official prejudice',
unequal matches were not 'inevitably deplored' (pp. 299–300).

The variety of attitudes to such marriages may be illustrated in three
generations of the same family. In 1514 Princess Mary (1496–1533),
the sister of Henry VIII, married Louis XII of France, who died in
1515. In the same year, as dowager Queen of France, she secretly
married Henry VIII's favourite, Charles Brandon, 1st Duke of Suffolk.
Neither partner was persecuted. Indeed, under the terms of Henry
VIII's will, their daughter Frances Brandon (1517–59) and her heirs
were included in the line of succession.

After Princess Mary's death the Duke of Suffolk married for the
fourth time. His wife, Katherine, bore him two sons, Henry (b. 1535)
and Charles (b. 1537/8). Their miniatures were painted at court by
Hans Holbein, and Henry was educated with Prince Edward (three
years his junior). Having succeeded to the title as 2nd Duke of Suffolk
in 1545, Henry carried the Orb at Edward VI's Coronation in 1547,
when he and his brother were both made Knights of the Bath. They
died of the sweating sickness in 1551, Charles having been 3rd Duke of
Suffolk for only half an hour.

Frances Brandon married, in 1535, Henry Grey, Marquis of Dorset.

Created Duke of Suffolk after her half-brothers' deaths in 1551, he was executed with their daughter, Lady Jane Grey, and her husband, Lord Guildford Dudley, for their part in Wyatt's rebellion, in 1554. Half a century after the widowed Duchess of Amalfi married her major-domo, the widowed Duchess of Suffolk married her secretary and groom of the chamber, Adrian Stokes, who was sixteen years her junior. Elizabeth I may have exclaimed, 'Has the woman so far forgotten herself as to marry a common groom!' but their portrait was painted by Hans Eworth in 1559, the year of the Duchess's death.

On the other hand, both the Duchess's surviving daughters, Lady Katherine Grey and Lady Mary Grey, who were at that time Elizabeth I's heirs, suffered imprisonment and separation from their husbands after contracting secret marriages. The Cardinal's cry

> Shall our blood?
> The royal blood of Aragon and Castile,
> Be thus attainted? (II.v.21–23)

is echoed in a recent comment on their fate: 'The Greys' only offence was that the dangerous blood royal flowed in their veins' (Maria Perry, *Elizabeth I: The Word of a Prince*, London: The Folio Society, 1990, p. 167).

Lower down the social scale, Dame Agnes Saunders, whose family was nevertheless wealthy enough to commemorate her in a monument in St Ethelreda's Church, Hatfield, married three times and had issue by each husband: see IV.ii.153–59n, p. 95 above.

III.i.66–78 As N.W. Bawcutt points out, Webster based this passage on Shelton's translation of Part I of *Don Quixote*, Book III, Chapter 8: '... onely I say now, that the assumpt or addition of a Witch, hath deprived me of the compassion I should otherwise have, to see those gray haires and venerable face in such distresse for being a Baude. Although I know very well that no sorcery in the world can move or force the will, as some ignorant persons thinke (for our will is a free power, and ther's no hearb or charme can constrain it.) That which certain simple women, or cousening companions make, are some mixtures and poysons, wherewithall they cause men runne madde, and in the meane while perswade us they have force to make one love well, being (as I have said) a thing most impossible to constraine the *Will*' (1612, pp. 195–96), ' "Don Quixote", Part I, and "The Duchess of Malfi" ', *MLR* 66 (1971), 488–91.

III.ii.110–12 Webster's source for these lines is Part I of *Don Quixote*, Book IV, Chapter 1: 'Then since herein I create no new world, nor custome, what error can be committed by embracing the honour wherewithall fortune crownes me?' (1612, p. 292, quoted by Bawcutt, ' "Don Quixote" and "The Duchess of Malfi" ', p. 489).

The identity of the madmen in Act IV, Scene ii

lines	Q1	Q4	Lucas	Fieler
74–77	1	Astrologer	Astrologer	Astrologian
78–80	2	Taylor	Lawyer	Lawyer
81–82	3	Parson	Priest	Priest
83–86	4	Doctor	Doctor	Doctor
87	1	Astrologer	Astrologer	Usher
88	2	Taylor	Lawyer	Taylor
89–91	1	Astrologer	Astrologer	Usher
92–93	3	Parson	Priest	Priest
94–95	1	Astrologer	Astrologer	Lawyer
96–97	2	Taylor	Lawyer	Farmer
98	3	Parson	Priest	Priest
99–100	4	Doctor	Doctor	Astrologian
101–2	1	Astrologer	Astrologer	Taylor
103–4	2	Taylor	Lawyer	Usher
105–7	3	Parson	Priest	Doctor
108–9	4	Doctor	Doctor	Farmer
110–11	3	Parson	Priest	Astrologian
112–13	4	Doctor	Doctor	Doctor

V.v.76–79 One source for the idea here expressed is found in Book III, Chapter 7 of Shelton's translation of Part I of Cervantes's *Don Quixote* (1612), where Quixote is discussing two kinds of lineage with Sancho Panza: 'Some that derive their pedigree from Princes and Monarkes, whom time hath by little and little diminished and consumed, and ended in a point like *Pyramydes* . . .' (quoted by N.W. Bawcutt, ' "Don Quixote" and "The Duchess of Malfi" ', p. 488). Another is found in Henry Peacham's *Minerva Britanna* (1612), p. 201, where a pyramid is depicted with the motto 'Minimus in summo', thus representing the ephemeral nature of greatness. The accompanying verse may also be connected with the death of the Cardinal, Bosola's vision of his own death and Delio's comment on 'wretched eminent things' (l.112): see Madelaine, 'Two Emblems', p. 147.

V.v.99–104, 119–20. Though such studies as Moody E. Prior's *The Language of Tragedy* (New York, 1947) and Robert Ornstein's *The Moral Vision of Jacobean Tragedy* (Madison, Wisconsin, 1960) find at times little or no connection between the play's sententiae and Webster's thought, Bosola's last words and Delio's final couplet receive considerable attention in discussions of the dramatist's philosophy. Interpretations of these passages vary considerably. For example, Lord David Cecil devotes his essay on Webster in *Poets and Storytellers*

(London, 1949), pp. 25–43, to an appreciation of the Christian basis of Webster's morality, and this argument has been amplified by two essays in *John Webster*, edited by Brian Morris, Mermaid Critical Commentaries (1970): Dominic Baker-Smith's 'Religion and John Webster' (pp. 205–28) and D.C. Gunby's '*The Duchess of Malfi*: A Theological Approach' (pp. 179–204: especially pp. 198–204). Other proponents of the view that Webster's final vision in the play is an expression of hope include Alexander W. Allison in 'Ethical Themes in *The Duchess of Malfi*', *SEL* 4 (1964), 263–73 and Bettie Anne Doebler, in 'Continuity in the Art of Dying: *The Duchess of Malfi*', *CompD* 14 (1980), 203–15. In 'The Case of John Webster', *Scrutiny* 16 (1949), 38–43, Ian Jack saw Webster as an unbalanced decadent, having no profound hold on any system of ethics. Gunnar Boklund, in '*The Duchess of Malfi: Sources, Themes, Characters*', pp. 128–35 and 164–70, sees the ending of the play as pessimistic. Wayne A. Rebhorn asserts that the claustrophobic vision of Act V is not Webster's last word on human experience, nor can one identify his point of view with Bosola's. Nevertheless, neither the Duchess's dignity nor her lingering presence can cancel out the play's strong impression of 'a diabolic and claustrophobic universe' (p. 61). Forker finds in the play a statement of 'tragic indeterminacy' (pp. 296–369), but concludes (p. 369):

> From one point of view the tragedy reflects the darker side of a perplexing but finally coherent universe; from the other it records the pathetic and courageous attempts of confused human natures to cope existentially with chaos. ... Such exaltation as Webster's greatest drama affords embraces the uncertainty and sees in it the measure of man's tragic dignity.

TEXTUAL APPENDIX

Variant readings which affect the verse structure of the play

NOTE: Editions published since 1963 have not been collated.

I.i

31–33 Qq print as verse.

35–54 [... *leave me*] Qq print as verse.

54–61 Q1 prints as verse; Q2, Q3, Q4 print as prose.

62–68 Q1, Q2 print as verse; Q3, Q4 print as prose.

I.ii

8–87 [... *Church,*] Qq print as verse.

87–89 Q1, Q2 print as verse; Q3, Q4 print as prose.

144 Sampson divides: ... *down/To the haven.*

153–54 Qq, Lucas print as prose; Dyce, Hazlitt, Vaughan, Sampson and McIlwraith print as verse.

155–56 Q1, Q2 print as prose; Q3, Q4 print as verse.

169–70 Qq, Dyce, Vaughan, Sampson, Lucas and McIlwraith print as one line. The division that I have adopted is that suggested by J.R. Brown in 'The Printing of John Webster's Plays (III)', *SB* 15 (1962), 63.

287b–88 Qq print as one line; Hazlitt divides: ... *excellence/* ... *you:/* ... *sake;/*; Dyce, Vaughan, Lucas and McIlwraith divide: *Beauteous?/Indeed* ...

289b–90 Qq divide: ... *the/Particulars* ...

309–10 Qq, Hazlitt, Sampson divide: ... *will./* ... *you/* ... *again./* Dyce and Vaughan read 'stranger' and divide as Qq. Lucas and McIlwraith divide: ... *will/* ... *strange/* ... *again./*.

II.i

1–47 Q1, Q2, Q3 and Hazlitt print as verse; Q4 cuts to three lines.

64–66 Dyce and Vaughan print as prose.

80–84; 90–96; 99–110 Qq and Hazlitt print as verse.

119–20 Brereton and Lucas divide: ... *troubled/With* ...

121–22 Brereton divides: ... *say/* ... *fore/ King./*.

148–49 Qq, Sampson and Lucas divide: ... *pretty/Art* ...; Dyce, Hazlitt, Vaughan and McIlwraith divide: *art,/This* ...

II.ii

1–27 Qq and Hazlitt print as verse.

35–36 Qq divide: ... *Switzer/In* ...; Lucas and McIlwraith divide:

... *even now/A Switzer* ...; Dyce, Hazlitt, Vaughan and Sampson print as prose.

39–42   Qq, Lucas and McIlwraith print as verse; Dyce, Hazlitt, Vaughan and Sampson print as prose.

II.iii

40–41   Qq divide: ... *well, sir./No, sir,/* ... *to't./.*

41b-42; 45–46   Qq print as one line.

44–48   Sampson divides: ... *name/* ... *sir,/* ... *safe./* ... *lying-in./* ... *not./.*

II.iv

10c-11   Qq and Hazlitt print as one line.

68–69   Qq divide: ... *that,/To my* ...

II.v

37   Qq, Dyce, Hazlitt and Vaughan print as two lines, dividing: *Thus/Ignorance* ...

50–51   Qq divide: ... *rage!/* ... *air/.*

III.i

87–88   Qq, Dyce, Hazlitt and Vaughan divide: ... *are/Your own* ...

III.ii

14   McIlwraith divides: ... *like her/The better* ...

68–69   Q1, Q2, Q3 and Hazlitt print as one line; Q4, Dyce *et al* divide: ... *tongue?/'Tis* ...

87–88   Qq divide: ... *I/Could* ...; Hazlitt divides: *Yes,/If I* ...

151–52   Qq, Dyce, Hazlitt and Vaughan divide: ... *action/Seem'd* ...

153–54   Qq, Dyce, Hazlitt and Vaughan divide: ... *him,/And so* ...

209–11   Q1, Q2 print as prose; Q3, Q4, Hazlitt and Brereton print as verse.

216–26   Qq print as verse; Brereton rearranges as verse.

266–68   Q1, Q2, Q3 print as two lines, dividing: ... *Politicians/* ... *heart string/*; Q4 *omits*.

271–72   Qq, Dyce, Hazlitt and Vaughan divide: ... *fall/Was* ...

312–14   Qq divide: ... *opinion/* ... *baths/* ... *Spa/*; Sampson divides: ... *hand./* ... *progress/* ... *Spa/.*

III.iii

12–13a   Q1, Q2, Q3 print as one line; Dyce, Hazlitt, Vaughan, Sampson and McIlwraith print as prose; Q4 *omits*. I follow Lucas in accepting this as verse.

40–46   Qq print as verse, dividing: ... *scholar,/* ... *was in/* ... *beard was/* ... *tooth-ache,/* ... *know the/* ... *this/* ... *man./.* Hazlitt prints as verse, dividing: *scholar,/* ... *was in/* ... *beard was,/* ... *troubled/* ... *tooth-*

ache/ . . . know/ . . . this/ . . . man./. Lucas rearranges the verse, dividing:
. . . scholar/ . . . knots/ . . . was/ . . . tooth-ache/ . . . know/ . . . shoeing-horn,/
. . . did/ . . . man./, but notes that the metre is 'very dubious'. Dyce,
Vaughan, Sampson and McIlwraith print as prose.

50–52   Qq print as verse, dividing: *. . . oppression/ . . . ones:/ . . . storm–/*;
Lucas prints as verse, dividing: *. . . oppression/ . . . ones/ . . . before/ . . .*
storm–/; Dyce, Hazlitt, Vaughan, Sampson and McIlwraith print as
prose.

54   Qq, Dyce, Hazlitt, Vaughan, Sampson and Lucas print as verse,
dividing: *. . . cannon/That . . .* McIlwraith prints as prose.

57–58   Qq, Hazlitt and Vaughan print as one line; Dyce and McIlwraith print as prose; Sampson and Lucas print as verse, dividing:
. . . whisper/Their . . .

59b–61   Sampson and Lucas print 59b–60 as one line; but Qq divide
60–61: *. . . fault, and/Beauty . . .*; Hazlitt divides: *That, that . . .*
her/Methinks . . . beauty/. I have followed the arrangement given by Dyce,
Vaughan and McIlwraith.

III.v

98–99   Qq and Hazlitt divide: *. . . me/Whether . . .*

105–6   Dyce, Vaughan and Sampson print three lines, dividing: *. . .*
heard/ . . . o'er/ . . . again./. McIlwraith has this division, but these are
two and a half lines in his edition.

108–9   Q1, Q2, Q3 and Hazlitt print as one line; Q4 omits 109.

IV.i

77–78   Qq and Sampson divide: *. . . mend/The . . .*; Dyce, Hazlitt,
Vaughan, Lucas and McIlwraith divide: *. . . bee/When he . . .*

94–95a   Dyce and Vaughan divide: *. . . pray–/No, . . .*

99b–100   Qq, Sampson, Lucas and McIlwraith print as one line; Dyce,
Vaughan and Brown divide: *. . . must/Remember . . .*; Hazlitt divides: *. . .*
remember/My . . .

107–8   Qq and Hazlitt print as one line.

IV.ii

37–38a   Qq, Dyce, Hazlitt, Vaughan and Sampson divide: *. . .*
now!/What . . .; Brereton, Lucas and McIlwraith divide: *. . . tragedy.*
/How . . .

83–113   Q1, Q2 print as verse; Q3, Q4 print as prose.

118–22   Lucas suggests the possible arrangement into verse, dividing:
. . . since/ . . . insensible/ . . . sure/ . . . I?/.

123–31; 133–38   Q1, Q2 print as verse; Q3, Q4 print as prose.

157–58   Qq divide: *. . . their/Minds . . .*; Hazlitt divides: *. . . but/As . . .*;
Sampson, Lucas and McIlwraith divide: *. . . but as/Their . . .* Dyce and
Vaughan print as prose.

357–59   In a note Sampson suggests the division: *. . . below/ . . .*

fountains/ . . . *up/* . . . *soul/* . . . *father/*. Lucas divides: . . . *below/* . . . *fountains/* . . . *living?/*.

362–64 Qq print as two lines, dividing: . . . *hence,/* . . . *deliver/*; Dyce, Hazlitt, Vaughan, Lucas and McIlwraith divide: . . . *Come,/* . . . *hence,/* . . . *deliver/*; Sampson divides: . . . *father./* . . . *hence,/* . . . *deliver/*.

V.i

37b–38a Brereton thinks that this should be one line.

V.ii

30–32; 40–43; 47–51 Qq and Hazlitt print as verse.

53–54 Dyce and Vaughan print as prose.

55–56 Qq and Hazlitt divide: . . . *mad/My* . . .; Sampson, Lucas and McIlwraith divide: . . . *lord?/Are* . . .; Dyce and Vaughan print as prose.

57–61 Qq divide: . . . *eye-/* . . . *civil./* . . . *him/* . . . *brought/* . . . *you/*; Hazlitt divides: . . . *off/* . . . *civil./* . . . *brought/* . . . *you/*; Sampson and Lucas divide: . . . *eyebrows/* . . . *civil/* . . . *him/* . . . *brought/* . . . *you/*; Dyce, Vaughan and McIlwraith print as prose.

65–66 Qq and Hazlitt divide: . . . *me/Now* . . .; Sampson and Lucas divide: . . . *begins/To* . . .; Dyce, Vaughan and McIlwraith print as prose.

68–80 Qq and Hazlitt print as verse.

164–65 Q1, Q2, Q3, Hazlitt and Sampson print as one line; Q4 *omits*.

171c–72 Qq, Hazlitt and Lucas print as one line.

197–98 Q1, Q2, Q3 and Hazlitt print as one line; Q4 divides: . . . *it./The Cardinal* . . .

205–6 Brereton says that these are really one line.

206–7 Dyce and Vaughan divide: . . . *need/Follow* . . .

227b–28 Sampson and McIlwraith print as one line.

231–34 Brereton rearranges the verse, dividing: . . . *love/* . . . *it?/* . . . *when you/* . . . *suspect/*.

267–68 Qq divide: . . . *your/Bosom* . . .; Hazlitt divides: . . . *you/Your* . . .

270c–71 Qq and Hazlitt print as one line.

282–83 Qq and Hazlitt divide: . . . *done,/I go,* . . .

289–90 Qq print as one line; Hazlitt divides: . . . *me/For* . . .

297 Qq, Hazlitt, Sampson and Lucas divide: . . . *more,/There is* . . .; Dyce, Vaughan and McIlwraith divide: . . . *there is/A Fortune* . . .

310–15 Qq and Hazlitt print as verse.

316–18 Dyce and Vaughan divide: . . . *remove/* . . . *out/* . . . *inquiry/*; Lucas divides: . . . *me/* . . . *body/* . . . *plague/*. I retain the Qq arrangement, as do Hazlitt, Sampson and McIlwraith.

320 Brereton would divide: . . . *Naples/To take* . . .

V.iii

33–34 Brereton retains the Q1, Q2, Q3 reading 'passes' and divides: . . . *passes of/Your* . . .

V.iv

35–37　Dyce, Vaughan and Sampson print as prose.

42b–43　Qq, Dyce, Hazlitt, Vaughan and Sampson divide: ... *prayers/There* ... I follow the division suggested by Brereton and adopted by Lucas and McIlwraith.

66–68　Brereton would divide: ... *good/* ... *preparative/* ... *ask/The* ...

70–71　Lucas suggests the division: ... *son/Fly* ...

V.v

7–8　Qq and Hazlitt print as one line; Dyce, Vaughan, Sampson and McIlwraith divide: ... *come?/Thou* ... Lucas divides: ... *me./Now? art* ...

12–13　Brereton thinks this should be one line.

16b–17　Qq, Dyce, Hazlitt, Vaughan and Sampson print as one line. I follow the division of Brereton, Lucas and McIlwraith.

33–35　Qq and McIlwraith print as two lines, dividing: ... *door/To* ...; Lucas prints as two lines, dividing: ... *unbarracade/The* ...

55–61　Q1, Q2 and Hazlitt print as verse; Q3, Q4 print as verse to ... *prosperity/* and give the rest of the speech in prose.

68b–69　Qq and Hazlitt print as one line.